Cooking Without Recipes

Cooking Without Recipes

By Philip Dundas

Illustrated by Robert Littleford

SPRING HILL

Published by Spring Hill, an imprint of How To Books Ltd
Spring Hill House, Spring Hill Road
Begbroke, Oxford OX5 1RX
United Kingdom
Tel: (01865) 375794
Fax: (01865) 379162
info@howtobooks.co.uk
www.howtobooks.co.uk

First published 2011

How To Books greatly reduce the carbon footprint of their books
by sourcing their typesetting and printing in the UK.

Text © 2011 Philip Dundas
Illustrations © Robert Littleford

British Library Cataloguing in Publication Data
A catalogue record of this book is available from the British Library.

ISBN: 978 1 905862 81 8

Produced for How To Books by Deer Park Productions, Tavistock, Devon
Designed and typeset by Mousemat Design Ltd
Printed and bound by in Great Britain by Bell & Bain Ltd, Glasgow

NOTE: The material contained in this book is set out in good faith for general
guidance and no liability can be accepted for loss or expense incurred as a result of
relying in particular circumstances on statements made in the book. Laws and
regulations are complex and liable to change, and readers should check the current
position with relevant authorities before making personal arrangements.

For HLIR, TC, CPBM and GOJ,
all of whom are my heroes.

Contents

Foreword by Simon Callow xiii

Introduction 1

Starting from Scratch 9

Tools of the Trade 11

Boiling Pans 12

Sauté Pan 13

Wok 14

Casserole 15

Knives 16

Chopping Board 19

Pestle and Mortar 20

Bowls 21

Wooden Spoons 22

Cleaning and Washing 23

A Miscellany of Implements 24

Useful Machines 25

The Kitchen Essentials 27

The Main Ingredients 27

Oil 28

Salt 31

Pepper 33

Lemons 34

Garlic 37

Using your Fridge 40

Stocking the Cupboards 43

Pulses and Grains 46

Vegetables 47

Fish 48

Fruit 50

The Carbs 51

Rice and Other Grains 52

Pasta and Noodles 53

Nuts and Seeds 54

Seasonings and Condiments 56

Adding Flavour 60

Working with Ingredients 63

Knife Skills 64

Preparing Vegetables 66

Root Vegetables 69

Potatoes 70

Onions, Shallots and Leeks 71

Beans 72

Peas 72

Brassicas 73

Tomatoes 73

Artichokes 74

Peppers 75

Aubergines 76

Mushrooms 76

Courgettes, Marrows and Cucumbers 77

Pumpkin and Squashes 78

Endive 78

Fennel 79

Preparing Seafood 79

Preparing Meat 84

Preparing Poultry and Game 91

Success in Your Kitchen 96

A Word About Heat 97

What Goes Together 100

Cooking for Friends 103

A Pot of Soup 104

Stock 106

Ingredients 109

Garnishes 112

Shaking Up a Salad 113

Dressings 116

Coming out of Its Shell 118

Lobster 121

Crab 122

Langoustines (Dublin Bay Prawns), Prawns and Brown Shrimp 122

Oysters 123

Mussels, Cockles and Clams 124

Scallops 124

Roast Dinners 125

Roasting Birds 128

Roasting Meat 131

Stews 134

Fishing Around 137

Fish Stew 142

Fish Pie 144

Risking a Risotto 144

Things on Toast 146

Perfect Pasta 149

A Little Offal 152

Stir-Fries 155

Vegetable Matters 157

Getting Saucy 159

The Cheese Board 162

Uncomplicated Puddings 164

Cooking Breakfast 168

A Survival Guide to Shopping 174

Cooks and their Books 179

Index 187

Foreword by
Simon Callow

My childhood was dominated by two remarkable grandmothers, as unlike each other as chalk and cheese. Both were superb cooks, but in radically different ways. One was French, with an accent that made Inspector Clouseau look like an effortless polyglot; the other German in origin, but with a particularly beautiful, very English voice. Oddly enough, the French grandmother, Toto, was in her element cooking traditional English dishes (roast beef, Yorkshire pudding, custard), which never varied by an iota, whereas the other one – well, that's where Cooking Without Recipes comes in. The other one, Mater, never read a recipe in her life, instead producing an endless variety of completely original dishes according to her whim or what happened to be in the cupboard or the fridge.

My aunt, who lived with her, made sure that there was always a good stock of standard and not-so-standard ingredients to hand, and Mater would – generally at the very last moment – sweep in to the kitchen and say, 'What have we got, then?'. Twenty minutes later, something extraordinary would appear on our plates. To achieve this, the rest of us were required to become hyperactive *commis* chefs, as she threw out instructions: 'peel this!', 'slice that!', 'boil some water, boy, quick!'. As a result, of course, I never really knew how anything had been made. It was a kind of culinary conjuring trick, dazzling but incomprehensible.

As time went on and I left home, I lived in the usual sordid student accommodations and barely attempted to cook anything other than baked beans and omelettes. By great good luck, the guy with whom I lived at drama school was a fine cook, then when I started acting, much of my life was spent on tour or in B&Bs. As time went on, one relationship succeeded another. The only thing these men of mine had in common was – whether by luck or design – that they were all very good cooks. I didn't need to cook and, frankly, I was too daunted by their brilliance to attempt to serve up my fumbling offerings for consumption. And then finally I met someone who couldn't cook at all and rather expected me to. I was terrified, and immediately bought twenty cookbooks, which I followed slavishly. To my astonishment, the results were edible. Sometimes, they even tasted like proper food. This, I concluded, was because I had followed the instructions to the letter.

And then came the great day when I forgot to get a crucial ingredient. People were due in a couple of hours; I had to start cooking almost immediately; I was on my own. So I improvised. I ran across to the little grocery store and got what I hoped and prayed would work. In the end it turned out rather better than what I'd planned. This was the beginning of liberation. I started using recipes as a mere matrix for dishes. I admit, though, to never having quite abandoned them. It takes the courage and confidence of a Dundas to see them simply as entertaining culinary diversions.

I met Philip about five years ago, and before long he started murmuring his dangerous but liberating philosophy into my ear: 'the kitchen is a playground,' he would say. 'There are no rules.' 'Follow your instincts.' 'If it works, it's okay.' 'Just make it up.' This was rather radical stuff, the equivalent of a culinary bra burning. I was greatly encouraged when he invited me to eat at his table – fantastic, unprecedented things would materialise without having seemed to have been cooked at all. Of course, like any artist who seems supremely relaxed – Fred Astaire, Picasso, both of whom he resembles, in different ways – the effortless result is the outcome of years of thought and experiment and practice. *Cooking Without Recipes* doesn't tell you that you don't have to work at it – it just liberates you from the tyranny of someone else's culinary imagination. Do your own thing, it says, listen to the food, pay regard to your stomach and your palate, let cooking become second nature.

It is the book my grandmother would have written if she had known how to frame a sentence, which Philip certainly does. Read, inwardly digest, then throw the book away. This is the first day of the rest of your life in the kitchen.

Simon Callow

Introduction

When my dad died he was described by an old friend thus: 'so sartorial, such a thinker and dreamer of impossible dreams, and a teller of tales...the ideal of everyone's uncle – kind, concerned and always up to giving one a very good lunch!'

Dad loved 'grub'. But he was one of the most particular people I ever met and a creature of habit. In the 36 years I knew him, every morning he had a soft floury roll baked in the top oven of the ancient Aga for a few minutes and rather lavishly buttered, followed by two oatcakes with Dark Breakfast marmalade and Indian tea without milk, preferably stewed a little in a metal teapot on the hot plate. On special occasions, he might have some extremely crispy bacon. He loved everything slightly burned. The top of a rice pudding, toast, the skin of a chicken, onions and so on. A taste I have inherited.

As an eligible bachelor in the 1950s he was the heart's desire of a bevy of dazzling county beauties. He'd invite them for lunch or supper a bit early and then get them to cook for his other guests. Best of all, he'd be invited to shoot at house parties where he'd be spoiled as he had been by his mother. Heavy puddings, cakes and vast, unending breakfasts.

Like most men of his generation he couldn't cook and his tastes were incredibly conservative. Thin wafers of ox tongue, steak and kidney pie and very well hung, almost maggoty game were his favourites. During the Second World War he had served in the North West Frontier of India, but of course despite the dust and artillery shells, mess dinners were as British as possible – always served on regimental china and eaten with silver knives and forks. The smell of curry struck fear in his heart.

Later at Cambridge, nursery food was his mainstay – game soup, Beef Wellington and sponge puddings. And of course it was in plentiful supply at his various London clubs. But after he married, that all changed. My mother was more adventurous; a disciple of that dangerous radical Elizabeth David. She would try to feed him 'revolting foreign muck' such as cheese, salads and pasta dishes.

Dad was my adopted stepfather and he was a bully. And my extrovert precocity infuriated him. But we shared one thing. Like me, he was greedy. So I knew just how to exact my revenge against his extreme punishments. On the farm, there was a gardener, Walter, who oversaw the kitchen garden and Dad's pride and joy – his orchards and greenhouses. There were espalier apricots and pears against roughcast East Lothian sandstone, white muscatel grapes and figs under glass, nectarine houses and asparagus in cloches, heated with lead wires in the ground. From redcurrants to his sacred Royal Sovereign strawberries, they were gardens of which Ceres herself would have been justly proud. Walter was always in a cloth cap and wearing a slightly upturned smile, kneeling and trudging round the garden like a guard, viewing my presence with disapproval, protecting his perfectly sweet young peas from my marauding hands.

In the early mornings my father would wander with Walter through the greenhouses or past the apple trees checking for the perfect ripeness of his latest progeny. As any gardener will know, each fruit carries a 'bloom', a sort of musty blush, which must be unsullied for the perfect finish. Soon he began to recognise an earlier predator at his prizes. Little finger marks on the bloom betrayed a thief among the nettings and glass. Just before he was ready to pluck a succulent nectarine from the tree, it vanished. I would be sitting on a wall or the branch of a tree, juice dripping down my chops, anticipating the fury awaiting me. I remained undeterred. Dad loved chocolate too and hid boxes of expensive truffles from London around his private spaces in the house. I knew them all. And stole my place among his private gluttony, feasting on the spoils.

So he carried on for years and survived life's hills and sharp corners. Then my adopted mother died. Ironically, from malnutrition caused by cancer of the bowel. She was a Christian Scientist and had told no-one of her pain. We had been estranged, on and off, for many years and I had left home as a teenager. But all the same, I went back to look after Dad. A few days turned into weeks and an uneasy peace settled between us. We both knew I had been done wrong. This was our opportunity to make some quiet restitution.

One day I arrived to find him in the kitchen trying out his first purchase since the funeral – an ice cream churn. No fuss, just two bars of dark chocolate and a pint of double cream. He ate it with brandy snaps and caster sugar sprinkled on top.

Those were Dad's final few months at home. And they were relatively happy ones. And I fell for his youthful charm, encouraging that new-found independence. He was reclaiming territory around the house from which he'd long been banished by my, sometimes, rather brutal mother. Funniest of all, he was a complete stranger to the kitchen. Certainly, he'd spent many hours in this room, eating his meals and lecturing small boys on the virtues of honesty, labour and Greek grammar. But he had never really any idea of what went on there. So, in his eager curiosity for everything new, he lost no time and asked me to teach him how to cook all of his favourite things.

We started with soup and then roast potatoes in goose fat. Apple pie, omelette, lamb stew and mince came next. His biggest triumphs were Scotch broth with a real mutton bone, roast partridge and rhubarb crumble with home-made custard. Each took a few failed attempts and considerable carnage around a previously spotless kitchen. But what he acquired was a confidence born of necessity. He taught himself to shop, started reading food writers and once he even cooked for friends.

Having lost all the women who cooked for him and being too old to acquire a new model, he briefly became a reconstructed modern man, ready for jolly new adventures in the kitchen. And he was an eager pupil, learning fast and fearlessly. He even became more interested in ingredients he had always dismissed. Things that were completely alien to him such as lentils, garlic, olive oil, herbs and pasta weirdly fascinated him. He'd talk almost childishly with regret about how he had dismissed Indian food and the 'blasted beastly smell of it'. But having read about the spice trade, a whole world of ancient history opened up to him. And as a scientist, he loved Heston Blumenthal and wanted to understand the 'how' of cooking, the reactions of heat and taste. Most of all he wanted to master cooking for himself.

Poor Dad didn't last long enough to do this. He was invited by his brother on a cruise. Not a worldly man, he had imagined sailing to Madeira in the 1940s with his sweetheart, when everyone dressed for dinner. He duly appeared on the first evening in a 16oz barrathea dinner jacket and silk facings. The rest of the passengers were in shirt sleeves and sandals. He felt a figure of fun like Mr Pooter in *Diary of A Nobody*, suffering the snobbish indignity of meeting the local tradesmen at the Lord Mayor's Ball. Most of all he missed my mother. On the third day he retired very sick to his cabin, refusing to answer the door. I think this is when he relinquished his hold on life. He reappeared when the ship docked at Southampton ten days later, a sick man and spent the rest of his days in a nursing home, returning to the farm one last time.

Ensconced in his nursing home, as Dad went into decline he became more obsessed with reading about food. We talked a lot and I read him the articles from my blog 'PipsDish' at his bedside. He encouraged me to write from the perspective of people who loved ingredients but didn't want to follow recipes; a light read in the loo during a morning constitutional or in bed before dropping off to sleep, as if somehow in his dreams he might acquire the abilities to concoct all those dishes he loved.

He would order me to make him things he had read about, such as quince crumble and dressed crab. And I would find packages at his bedside from Amazon with the latest offerings from the food publishers. But the greatest surprise of all was that after 60 years of being a staunch dyed in the wool right-wing Daily Telegraph reader, one day he announced disparagingly, 'I am simply bored of reading what I already know' and promptly switched to the Guardian. For the food writers.

And thus came *Cooking Without Recipes*. It aims to do all the bits that most cookery books overlook by consigning the most useful information to a few pages at the beginning or between chapters. These are the essential bits of knowledge you need to become a confident and creative cook because they liberate you. When you know which pan to own, or what to do with a fish once you've got it home, how to buy the right kind of knife, how to actually use fresh sage without it overpowering, or make a salad dressing, how to knock something together from the old remnants of your fridge, then you become free of constraints.

This book just helps you start that journey. It's about helping you to achieve your simplest ambitions in the kitchen, bringing alive the possibilities of food, helping you become happier, more confident and creative in the kitchen. It does not contain exhaustive lists of techniques for scrambling eggs or detailed skills for particular styles of cooking; it has no aspirations to tell the reader how to become the baking goddess. But it will help you work out how to make almost anything you want to eat.

It will encourage you to find new ways to shop for, cook and eat the kind of food you love – something you may have thought was only possible for foodie experts. From creating a kitchen space you enjoy being in and clearing cupboards of unwanted debris to stocking them with essential ingredients and preparing and cooking them in ways you like, this book will give you confidence in the kitchen.

From what you can do with herbs, oils and sauces to enrich what you fancied in the fishmonger's window, to acquiring the art of using imaginatively what is left over from a meal, this is a manual of kitchen life for anyone who adores good food and wants to share the love.

All confident, passionate and experienced cooks have some things in common. They love their kitchens and know their ingredients. They decide how to prepare a dish using their imaginations as well as their culinary skills. For them, cooking is a labour of love, something in which they can lose themselves. By acquiring a calm attitude to cooking food and eating it, with only a pot, a pan, a knife and a spoon, you too can beat the fear of the unknown and become creative in your own kitchen.

Of course, recipes books are rich seams of knowledge and often showcases for flamboyant creativity. They are sources to mine for ideas and inspiration but very few actually teach you how to cook.

This book focuses on the skills and ideas that will help you learn without making you feel intimidated by complicated dishes or exotic ingredients, at the same time as offering all sorts of ideas for cooking which will test and develop anyone's abilities.

When you understand the principles of cooking certain things, you can go it alone. After my mother's death, the only thing my father wanted to know was how to make Scotch broth. To him it was a mystery until he understood the simplicity of making stock, soaking the broth mix and chopping up a few vegetables to go in. And once he knew the principles of soup-making, others followed. He became an expert. This book is based on learning those simple principles.

If you want to learn to cook, you must first learn to understand ingredients rather than read recipes. Otherwise you will achieve nothing but cooking by numbers. Secondly, cooking is about confidence and creativity, two things you have to look for within yourself. Only picking up a fish by the tail will tell you how to cook it.

Thirdly, if you have no affection for your ingredients, your efforts will be rendered inedible. Bring to the surface what lies within, entice the senses and please the appetite without unnecessary embellishment or distraction. And lastly, your mood will determine the success of your undertaking. Successful cooking is to satisfy completely both yourself and those who will eat your food, with comfort and ease.

So this book is dedicated to those who want to learn the behaviours and habits of a cook, so that they can choose any ingredient and in turn become inventive, self-reliant and take control in their own kitchens.

As long as I can remember, I wanted to be a writer and for the same amount of time, I have loved food and cooking. But it took me a long time to actually recognise that I could usefully bring both passions together. Writing a book about food today is one thing, getting it published is a long shot. I want to acknowledge a few important people who have coaxed and cajoled this work from me. The first is Helen Runciman, my soul-mate, with whom – from collecting vegetables from her father's kitchen garden to drinking mint juleps at The Ritz – I shall treasure some of the most dramatic, delicious, inebriated, expensive and truly awful culinary memories. Simon Callow, loyal friend, gastronome and *bon viveur*, has given unfailing ear and eye to this endeavour, both as pupil and enthusiast. He knows more about everything than anyone I know, as well as continually bringing genius and generosity to the stage and page. Melissa Bakewell, who is simply the best cook I know, and my big sister Emma who gave me the family I dreamed of.

I owe Jasmine Gartner much for taking the time to peruse and edit the early versions of this book. And thanks are due to Beth Coates, Pete Irvine and Jamie Jauncey, who each in their own way helped me to find my voice. Nikki Read and Giles Lewis for publishing me and telling me that reading the book made them want to cook again. My newest friend and collaborator, Robert Littleford, who was the first person to read the book from cover to cover and immediately wanted to illustrate it. I look forward to many future adventures with him in words and pictures.

Glynn, who some will know from my blog as 'the Belgian' reckons he taught me everything I know. He certainly eats everything I cook. For that and many, many other reasons I love him with all my heart.

There are many others who have fed and been fed by me over the years. I thank you all and hope you'll find something you taught me or learn something you wanted to know from this book.

Starting from Scratch

For a number of reason, kitchens can be quite scary places. You might have inherited one from someone else or you may suddenly be faced with a new responsibility to use this as a room in which to actually cook something. You might be a virgin – hugely keen but profoundly inexperienced – which means you previously just walked past this room blushing hoping it wouldn't notice you, or perhaps rushed in terrified, made a cup of coffee and fled.

You may have moved into a new flat and find yourself looking into a strange cupboard-like room in the centre of your new home, with no air or light and some barely functioning appliances dating back to the 1970s. For others still, it's just a place designed by someone else for an activity you don't really understand; a room you've entered for years solely to be served your daily food intake.

Whatever your experiences of kitchens, take heart. As long as you love eating food and either want or need to start cooking for yourself, this room is about to become your refuge: a place to shrug off the daily grind, where you will find nourishment in body and soul. And just maybe, it will eventually become your very own studio, a place of creativity and experiment.

So, here you are. Possibly with new eyes for the kitchen, or in it alone for the first time. It can be quite a confusing room, full of drawers and cupboards containing machinery and inexplicable implements that look like instruments of medieval torture. Most of this paraphernalia is entirely unnecessary. And without someone around who knows what to do with these contraptions, the best approach is to select the basic tools you will need for your planned activities in the kitchen. As for the rest, leave well alone.

Most kitchens contain a combination of useless, new-fangled and ancient stuff, acquired over years, used infrequently and left to gather rust and grease. If you are starting out in your first flat or you face a virgin kitchen with nothing in it and completely unlike anything you have seen before, it will probably seem pretty daunting. In fact, you are the lucky one. You can start afresh with exactly what you need and no more.

The first thing to ensure in this case is that you resist any attempts by well-meaning relatives to offload unwanted kitchen flotsam upon you. They will doubtless have boxes of cooking detritus in attics and basements which they themselves have inherited. And seeing an opportunity to 'clear out', imagining they are doing you a good turn, will try to make you the unwilling recipient of long obsolete and perfectly useless items.

Having said this – a note of caution. It is never wise to upset a doting relative. If you are leaving home, they will doubtless be mourning the sad prospect of your loss and cooking for one less hungry mouth. Rather than dismissing their generosity out of hand, explain gently that you have already decided what you need but that you'd love to have a look to see if there is anything you've missed. Indeed you may find that there is a glamorous set of china, cutlery or glassware. These are always useful and will save you considerable expense later. But be aware that when that fateful day arrives when you find someone to join forces with you, they may not share your enthusiasm for old family heirlooms.

Tools of the Trade

It's easy to fill a kitchen with things you don't need. But to become skilled in uncomplicated cooking, you really only need a small amount of simple, quality equipment. In truth, there are only a few essential items for cooking: a pan, a knife, chopping board, pestle and mortar, and a bowl are all the neophyte kitchen god needs to get going. Add to the list perhaps another pan, an ovenproof dish and a couple of wooden spoons and you are pretty much in business.

Of course, this slightly over-simplifies the matter for those who are more ambitious and it does depend on what style of cooking you are going to favour. If you want to become a baker *extraordinaire*, you'll need different equipment. For our purposes, these basic tools are a good place to start.

An important piece of advice. This goes for lots of things in life as well as cooking. If you spend money on buying the top-notch, you'll spare yourself trouble later.

Boiling Pans

Most of us have a set of pans we've been given, bought or that just seem to have attached themselves to our lives. Yours may have followed you loyally from home to home and be etched with the experiences of your life. But their quality will vary hugely and the last thing a cook needs is rattling pans with loose handles and ill-fitting lids. Now is the time to treat yourself to something new. And a bit like a pair of gloves or a well-tailored overcoat, it's really best to buy your own so that you know you have a perfect fit.

Top-quality pans are works of technical precision with many layers of different metal to ensure the best performance. The main features to look out for in a pan are weight, handle and lid. Heaviness is the most important, even if it makes the vessel more cumbersome to lift. Something with a solid bottom is essential as it retains heat longer and allows for more balance and control; basically so it doesn't tip over and you don't burn yourself. There is nothing more terrifyingly pregnant with disaster than a flimsy pot full of boiling water, wobbling on the hob.

Next, the right kind of handle is vital. One should always be wary of small pans with handles on the side. Pay particular attention here. Check the rivets. Do they look secure or might you end up with a few litres of scalding stock on your feet? Handles should be sturdy and solid, never hollow. You'll be needing a firm grip, especially when pouring away boiling liquids. A pour spout on the rim of a pan is a useful feature, and the best ones also have draining holes in the deep inner lip of the lid. You may have to buy the lid separately. Make sure it fits snugly.

You can easily manage with one decent-sized pan at least thirty centimetres in diameter. You should spend money and get something that looks as if you could live in it, if everything goes wrong. It should be a capacious cauldron. Think of something in which you can see yourself boiling a ham or making pasta for a multitude of friends.

This size will give you scope and possibilities. It's functional and you'll be able to do everything from soup to the more adventurous things such as stirring up your very own marmalade.

For convenience, you will also be able to use a large bamboo vegetable steamer (available from Chinese supermarkets), which will fit over the top. And when you've finished cooking, your pan will even double as a washing up bowl by throwing into it all your dirty implements, while you enjoy eating.

Sauté Pan

Next you need a less deep but wide sauté pan, about 25–35cm across. You'll be using this for so many different purposes: cooking fish and meat dishes, vegetables, eggs and bacon, croûtons, sauces, risottos – the list is endless. So once again, it has to be something that looks good and that you will really treasure, something you can serve from directly at the table without wasting any precious juices and flavours. You don't need a lid with a sauté pan. But it is important to find one with no plastic in the handle, so that you can move it into the oven or push it under the grill to finish things off. Some pans now use a silicone-rubber in the handles which seems to work fine under high temperatures and lends extra grip. You'll notice that professional cooking pans have long handles. It is always best to create distance between you and hot things, especially when dealing with boiling water and spitting oil.

If you really want the best and can afford it, then pans with a copper seam in the bottom are the cook's dream. Copper conducts heat well and so it's easier to regulate the exact temperature you want, which helps you be more in control of your cooking. Actual copper pans cost a king's ransom and aren't strictly necessary for the home cook but they look fantastic.

If you have Le Creuset pans, then these will stand you in good stead. They are expensive, but for good reason: because they last for years. Some of mine were inherited and one is at least 40 years old. But they do need to be used. So often one sees in people's kitchens these iconic orange and blue pans teetering on the top of kitchen shelves, inexplicably kept in reserve for special occasions. Now is the time to make every day in the kitchen the best. After all, it might be your last meal.

Wok

Stir-frying generally is a godsend and the best thing to use is a wok. To be able to slice up a few vegetables, anything really, and throw them in a pan with some meat or fish, herbs and sloshes of soy sauce is a smart way to cook. And because it's so fast, you don't lose the valuable nutrients that more invasive cooking can destroy. A wok will provide you with the easiest, quickest and most nourishing of suppers – perfect for the novice cook.

You can buy the most functional versions from Asian supermarkets. They are made of steel (not stainless) so you shouldn't wash them with soap. Just clean them with water and wipe with a bit of cooking oil after use. There is a trick known as seasoning, which involves coating the inside with oil and heating up the wok until it smokes. It burns a layer of oil on to the surface of the wok, but you need to keep repeating the process every so often. And if the wok does get a bit rusty, set to with a wire scourer and then oil it up again. Unfortunately, although you can find hybrids, woks only work really well with gas.

Casserole

Originally the French word for 'saucepan', as with the words tandoori and tagine in English, we have ascribed the word casserole to the type of food that was cooked in it, *en casserole*.

Basically we are talking about any ovenproof dish. You have to discover what you like using best but whatever it is, it should be fit for the table. The experience of eating should always be accompanied by an aesthetic pleasure. Why keep ugly cooking dishes? That's like people who put their least attractive furniture and university posters in their spare bedrooms. Surely you want to show off your exquisite taste all the time?

The most practical ovenproof casseroles are the earthenware dishes you can buy in Spain and Portugal and now in many cook shops. They are functional, cheap to replace and look stylish from oven to table. They are hugely versatile and will sustain high temperatures, although you probably shouldn't put them directly over a flame or pour cold water on them when hot, as they might crack.

You can use your Le Creuset pans in the oven but there are now a range of covered roasting dishes on the market. These look like large saucepans made of highly durable, conductive and often non-stick materials. These are ideal if you want to start something off on the hob, *pot au feu* style, such as a pheasant or duck, and then transfer them to the oven. They also have lids, which means that you can preserve moisture and flavour. Using them also saves you from one of life's most unpleasant and unrewarding activities: cleaning the inside of an oven.

Knives

Once you have your basic receptacles, the most important consideration in the kitchen (after ensuring that there is a decent bottle of wine within reach) is to find the perfect knives with which to arm yourself.

However, what you generally find available to purchase in the way of cutting tools should rightly fill you with horror. You don't need to be a trained chef to see the dangers inherent in those wobbly, blunt, serrated blades lurking in every kitchen drawer. If you don't spot a bad knife early, you'll have plenty of scars to prove it later.

You can only mitigate against these perils by choosing the best knives money can buy. You need to combine domestic good sense with honed hunter-gatherer instincts in the careful selection of the right ones. You'll see professional chefs using endless different knives, but a kitchen knife, a paring knife and a honing steel are more than enough at home.

A kitchen knife should be like your favourite pair of shoes: comfortable, reliable and strong. And you can even follow exactly the same process when buying one. Go to a shop where will let you have a 'fitting'. What you are looking for is a stainless steel cook's knife. They are easily identifiable from the handle. This should be in two parts, preferably wooden, divided by what is called the tang, and riveted together. The tang is the alloy shaft that secures the knife to the handle. On a well-made knife, this should equal the length of the blade. You'll want the knife to be between sixteen and thirty centimetres.

Carbon steel requires less sharpening but is less malleable and can taint certain foods such as fish and fruit. For your purposes, stainless steel is perfect and moves with you over the years, adapting to your hand in subtle ways like the nib of a fountain pen.

This is going to be a long partnership, so make sure you buy judiciously. Think about the sorts of food you eat. What will you need it for? Lots of meat will require a hefty blade whereas vegetarians might want something more agile. Then hold it firmly, like a confident handshake. Does it feel as though you don't want to let it go? With your palm facing up, balance the centre of the knife on your index finger. It should sit soft and stable in the hand.

You may also need a small paring or peeling knife for those fiddly jobs. Go for the same quality. Something about ten centimetres will do. And if you do have an old, small, blunt knife, keep it for preparing veg that needs close hand work.

The proper maintenance of a knife by keeping it sharp is about having respect for your food. You want to slice sheer, not hack. Shredding a cabbage, cutting down the spine of a fish or scoring across the grain of a lump of sirloin requires care and precision. That means having a loved and well-honed knife at the ready.

There is a common misconception about the sharpening of knives. Basically, as you use the knife, its fine edge, which is made up of microscopic metal fibres, is flattened. The best thing to correct this is to hone the blade using a steel, which doesn't actually sharpen but realigns these fibres.

If you have a friend who is a chef, ask them to show you how to use a steel. It is not difficult but you can damage the knife if you get it wrong, so it requires some practice. Hold the knife in your guiding hand, with your fingers round the handle and your thumb along the top. Hold the steel in your other hand across and away from your body.

Now, with the blade at twenty degrees to the steel, swipe each side gently down against it, exerting no pressure. The blade should just slide across the steel with a swishing sound. This should be repeated until you can feel that the edge of the blade is paper thin. Ideally, to keep the blade trim, you should do this each time you use the knife, then wipe the blade before using it.

Sharpening is another matter altogether and requires some skill. You should avoid electric or pull-through sharpeners as they attempt to do something like sharpen and hone at the same time and will wear your blade down very quickly. If you want to do your own sharpening, use a sharpening stone, which can be dry or sometimes lubricated with oil or water. At the same angle (twenty degrees), draw the blade across the stone, in the same direction for each side. Do this gently about ten times, then wash the blade. Even better than this, find a local butcher who will sharpen your knives (though be aware that the carrying of dangerous weapons is illegal in many places).

Chopping Board

The surface on which you cut and chop food should feel like a lumberjack's block: something solid, reliable and familiar. Although there are many kinds of board surface available, a general rule is that your board should never be harder than the blade. So definitely a no to glass or granite. The original butcher's blocks were made from really hard wood such as maple, and often assembled from pieces of timber with the grain upwards in order to create a strong cutting surface. In the old days, these would have been tree rounds, polished down and oiled. An apprentice butcher would acquire his block for a lifetime's work and keep on planing smooth the worn surface year after year.

Take the same attitude. You might start enjoying cooking and you will need to have something strong and practical at hand for all the jobs from decapitating a game bird to slicing a pumpkin.

Once again, when buying something for your kitchen, you get what you pay for. Source something solid and seasoned with as little glue involved as possible. Sometimes people just use end cuts from a wooden surface in a new kitchen. But don't get something so heavy you can't lift it.

Having several different boards is useful. If you get into baking, remember to keep a separate board because dough does have a habit of picking up any residue such as garlic or chilli – which is unpleasant in a birthday cake. You can also use boards to serve up food.

Quite rightly, there are fears in food preparation about encouraging nasty microbes like e-coli and salmonella. But solid wood has been proven to be highly effective in resisting these. As long as you are working with fresh ingredients and there are no pools of stagnant juices around, then the normal bacteria on wooden boards die off in a few minutes, whereas on plastic boards bacteria can actually multiply. Having said that, it's not a bad idea to keep a plastic board made from high-density polyethylene for cutting fish, garlic and bloody meat. Otherwise things can get smelly. And as aesthetics matter in your all-new kitchen, you want things to look and smell nice at all times. Whatever type of board you choose, both need thorough scrubbing after use.

Pestle and Mortar

This is one bit of kit that really does mark out the cook who wants to aspire beyond the mundane in the kitchen. It's the vessel of ancient magicians and priestesses, the tool in which the apothecary mixed his remedies, and the receptacle from which the alchemist hoped gold would emerge. It is the pestle and mortar.

These ancient companions are made of many different materials, from wood and brass to porcelain and glass. But you want a stone one, very hard, wide and deep. Nothing competes with this ancient way of pounding ingredients into submission. You'll just keep finding new uses for it all the time. With a pestle and mortar, you can have freshly bruised and cracked peppercorns to pep and draw out flavour in any dish. And this is just the beginning. You can crush garlic, salt and herbs to make marinades, dressings, spice mixes, salsas and even refreshing mixes for drinks like *caipirinhas* and fresh mint tea. Anything where you want to create driven flavours or merge ingredients into others.

Like the rest of the few important tools you now have in the kitchen, the pestle and mortar will become irreplaceable in your cooking life. You should start to treat it as such. Don't be too over-zealous in cleaning it. Like the way sherry and bourbon barrels insinuate themselves on maturing whisky, something of the magic in the next concoction you create will be inherited from what went before. A quick wipe or, if absolutely necessary, a rinse with hot water should be perfectly sufficient.

Bowls

As with so many kitchen necessities, we begin to know what we actually need as we do more cooking. But you will definitely have immediate use for an all-purpose bowl. The traditional brown ones you will have seen in many kitchens are called Faringdon but many of the celebrity chefs we see so much of have also launched their own lines of cookware. Their bowls tend to be excellent and are often sold in a set, which can be quite useful. If you prefer, you can also go for stainless steel bowls, which are easy to clean and have the advantage of being light.

But if you only buy one, you are looking for something deep and wide with gently inclining sides. Close your eyes and imagine enough room to get your hands deep, down and dirty. Fantasise about something large and curvaceous with a round bottom.

Once bowls are cracked or chipped, ditch them. Too many kitchens are full of charming but useless items which are hard to throw away, but they are just taking up much-needed space.

Wooden Spoons

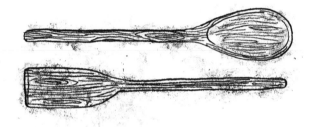

In the kitchen, wooden spoons are your friends. You need a fun and engaging collection. Small, tall, broad, frivolous, solid and seasoned hard wood. The latter is important because they are used for all sorts of stirring, squeezing, scraping, smoothing and seducing in cooking, from mayonnaise to meringues.

Like friends, as you go through life, keep hold of the ones you love but never tire of searching for new ones of the right calibre. Good ones that last are surprisingly hard to find. Once you've got them, it's worth the effort to treat them well. Don't machine wash them, as it removes the build up of oils that keeps them impervious to sauces, heat and colour.

Cleaning and Washing

The kitchen has become a focus of terror for the health and hygiene fanatic. The fear of invisible microbes and bacteria has led to a hysterical response towards cleanliness. This is reflected in the prevalence of cleaning potions and sprays that apparently kill off any protozoan life form in proximity.

Now the creative cook should be all for absolute cleanliness, but this is too extreme. Nasty organisms survive because they are given time to multiply. The problem is leaving dirty things lying around. You should never have to think of cleaning the kitchen, as you might other rooms in the house. All of your surfaces and implements must be treated with robust and continuous care as you are cooking.

If you go into a professional kitchen, you will never see a chef working in a midden of detritus and dirty vessels, and this is not only because they have someone to wash up after them. It's in a chef's nature to take what needs to be cleaned to the sink (for the lucky ones, someone else takes over from there) and wipe down the surface before starting to prepare the next dish.

Start by following simple rules in your kitchen and they will soon become second nature: wipe surfaces after each activity; have a linen glass cloth for all purposes; dispose of rubbish immediately; wash up while the water is hot. If you work to these principles, everything in life becomes simpler and you can enjoy eating without the burden of cleaning up hanging over you afterwards. And if you have a dishwasher, use it frequently so that it doesn't become a hostel harbouring unwanted smells.

Anything wooden should not be washed in soapy water as that will gradually remove the oils which build up in the wood and keep it seasoned. A thorough wipe or rinse under hot water should be followed by rubbing with a little oil on a piece of kitchen towel, the same treatment as you should give to a wok.

A Miscellany of Implements

Your kitchen is now tooled up. You are armed and ready to attempt anything from the most frugal to the most daring. However, there are a number of other items which, although they may not seem essential, will certainly make life easier.

Life without mashed potatoes is inconceivable, so make sure you have a masher. These implements seem to have been the subject of more than their fair share of redesigns but I have never found one to improve upon the standard model. You need a strong handle with a rounded end so that you can exert the right pressure and gusto to whip up a storm and achieve the perfect consistency.

Despite many imaginative attempts, there doesn't seem to be a grater from which your knuckles will be safe. Nonetheless having one is essential for three important activities: grating tomatoes, lemon zest and cheese.

A meat thermometer, digital or otherwise, is a boon. When you are cooking fabulous joints of meat or heavy poultry in the oven – whether it's fast and furious or low and slow – having a reliable check on the cooking temperature is sensible. While you can use a knife to slice into the meat, this allows all-important juices to escape and will reduce the succulence. And because meat continues to cook during 'resting' (after it has been taken out of the oven), you can overdo it with annoyingly disastrous consequences.

There remains a plethora of sieves, steamers, strainers, colanders, drainers, spinners, larders, spatulas and pipers you might want to have. Frankly, most will be fair-weather and unengaging kitchen acquaintances. But you choose them according to your mood. If they serve the moment, feel free. But you'll find that many of your time-served stalwarts will double-up remarkably well.

If your sieve will balance comfortably over your boiling pan, you can use it as an impromptu steamer or you could buy one of the cheap bamboo variety sold in Asian supermarkets. As a rule of thumb, a colander should be always big enough to hold whatever you are boiling in the pan. With a cloth over the top it's also ideal for shaking salad leaves dry.

Now that most of our kitchen appliances have timing mechanisms, you might not need a timer for eggs but if you do, they are less fiddly and they fulfil the golden rule of only doing one thing well. In this case, the perfect morning egg. A reflective moment in any cook's life.

Useful Machines

Cooking aids have advanced since the days of the Moulinex hand food mills. But the staggering range of what is available often belies their usefulness in the kitchen. You can have every variety of mixer, juicer, blender, whizzer and processor. Some machines do all of these tasks; others, in a rather superior and expensive fashion, do only one.

The best invention of the last twenty years is the hand blender. Inexpensive, convenient and blissfully simple, you just take it to the pot and press the button. Soup just became the easiest thing in the world. And they can also be used for many other brilliant activities in the kitchen.

A food processor is useful too but only the main bowl and the big knife. Machines with endless attachments that frappé ice, shred beans and julienne carrots are maddening to clean and are infuriatingly difficult to store.

There are also a number of machines that even cook for you, such as steaming rice, grilling, steaming or baking bread. That's fine if you have the space and no interest in how the food emerges. But the fuss never seems to balance with the efficiency or the outcome. Posh food mixers are like Agas: they look impressive but they are for people who have huge kitchens and nothing else to do all day but bake.

If you are a coffee drinker, then an electric grinder is essential kit (it can also be used for grinding spices). Coffee beans have the same properties as peppercorns and suffer equally from maltreatment. Minutes after the coffee bean is split, the flavours of the oily compounds that give this drink its compulsive divinity begin to dissipate and the taste is lost. If you only grind what you need to use and do so immediately, all the aromas return in the cup to give you that unmistakably rich elixir that is freshly ground coffee. Which is why coffee shops have become so successful. Once you've tried this at home, you'll soon find that you eschew all other manifestations.

The Kitchen Essentials

The first lesson for anyone reclaiming a kitchen as their own is to throw everything out and start again. Just like the kitchen equipment we discussed in the previous chapter, only keep the basics: in this case, the ingredients that make up the dishes you like to eat. This way you can immediately cultivate a relationship with your kitchen where you can walk into it anytime, knowing that there is an arsenal of supplies from which you can whistle up something to eat. Whether you are a frantic businesswoman, a media mogul, a struggling actor, a secret agent or catwalk model, you'll learn to rely on your own instincts to cook what you want to eat, when you want to eat it.

To achieve this level of efficiency, there are just few things you need to have in your cupboards: seasonings and oils to bring the best out of vegetables, meat and fish in cooking; dried foods like rice, pasta and pulses to accompany your dishes; and a few decent products in tins and jars, handy at a moment's notice to make life easier as well as offering you some interesting choices. Last but not least, you'll need wine, an invaluable friend in the kitchen for drinking and cooking.

The Main Ingredients

Having staples in stock all the time means we can throw together that spontaneous supper for a colleague from work or an impulse date from nothing but fresh air, an anchovy and a squeeze of lemon. And most staples will last for months, though you don't want to keep them so long that the weevils get them or the tins explode.

There is also a distinct difference between what we need to have at the ready and what just takes up essential space. When compiling kitchen staples, think tactically as though you were collecting the essential elements of a medicine cabinet or an adventure survival kit. And that's not far wrong. These bare essentials of cooking are themselves the very basic elements of creation.

Oil

The first thing you will need in the kitchen is the best extra virgin olive oil. It's not hard to understand how the liquid sun distilled from the humble olive was the basis for the fine unguents of ancient history. Used to salve wounds of war and assuage angry gods, this commodity has been the mainstay of trade across nations and

continents for centuries. But surprisingly, it didn't really become popular in Britain until the 1980s. Thankfully the best oil is here to stay, and a good thing too – both for our hearts and our taste-buds.

Oil is fat and we all need some fat of the right sort in our diet. And the good news is that you can use oils for everything from cooking to salads, or even just sprinkling over bread or soup to give it a bit of flavour.

But if you look in food shops or supermarkets, you will be faced with a staggering variety of oils. And each of them produced with different levels of quality, from the quaintly artisanale to the mass manufactured. Some are pricey and others are tasteless. Some cook well and others are better unheated. Where to begin?

Understanding olive oil can be a confusing business, but producing olive oil is very similar to wine-making. Though there are many varieties of olive grown in different areas, it is only really what is done to them after they are harvested that makes a difference to the oil you buy. Like grapes, they are pressed, and what is extracted is of differing quality depending on that process. The purest, unadulterated 'extra virgin' olive oil comes from the first pressing of one harvest and is pressed on stone mills that cannot crush the stones or pips. This means that the oil has low acidity and more subtle flavours.

All other olive oils are mechanically produced and the flavours are chemically stabilised. This product, which can be described as 'pure olive oil', becomes part of a blend, just like blended wine. It's not necessarily the worse for it, but will be more suited to different purposes. The rule is to avoid what are called 'pomace', 'refined' or 'blended' oils; they are mass produced and undergo an extraction process to remove acidity which, by default, purges the delicate flavours.

Like choosing wine, you need to be selective. And like coffee, tea and flour, when you use the best, nothing compares. Because you can buy so many different kinds of olive oil, it's worth experimenting, using it in any way you like. Some ingredients respond well to being doused, others require the lightest touch. You will be well served by any bottle or tin with 'virgin' or 'extra virgin' on the label. Although many would argue that extra virgin olive oil doesn't respond well to high temperatures and so you might use a pure olive oil for sautéing.

But like everything in the kitchen, there are no rules, you should simply follow your instinct. The very finest oils are perfect with the merest hint of salt and soaked up in bread. The more robust can be used for pretty much anything. You learn your own way. Taste and experience are your only guides.

In truth, there isn't much you can't do with olive oil (and butter). But, having said that, in time you may want to experiment using different varieties of oil, depending on what you are doing with them.

Use sunflower, or grapeseed and rapeseed, oil for hot frying, shallow or deep. They have what is known as a higher 'smoke point' (which is the point when the oil is literally burning, the flavours are reduced and it's rendered useless, as well as highly flammable). These lighter oils are less oleaginous and therefore break down more easily.

Toasted sesame oil is worth experimenting with and brings a smoky Eastern flavour to any dish.

Walnut oil is a delicate joy in salads and high in essential fatty acids.

A word of warning: generally avoid anything generically named 'cooking oil'. It is produced like margarine in a rather unpleasant, high-intensity blending process called hydrogenation. And, like the palm and coconut oils that are used in processed foods, cooking oils are dangerously high in unhealthy saturated fats.

Salt

Salt is a much-maligned compound. It's true that too much of it can be harmful, but absence of beneficial salts can be equally bad for you so, as with so many things, a healthy balance is advisable. Like many food staples, this ingredient goes back to the dawn of time. The essential curative properties of salt made it a powerful commodity in global trade, and to this day curing and salting are still common ways of preserving all sorts of foodstuffs in many cultures.

We need salt in our systems to survive and it is a vital ingredient on your cooking palette board. Not only does it help to cause reactions in cooking, it also gives necessary edge to some dishes. On the other hand, we must be careful. The over-use of highly refined salt, and the chemically produced salts in manufactured foods, are dangerous and can cause serious heart problems.

Salt comes refined and unrefined. Naturally, the latter is vastly superior for flavour, is better for you and is so easily available that there is no reason to buy the chemically produced version. Sea salt is the most common, collected in areas of naturally enclosed sea water, called salt flats, beds or pans. Seasonally, as the water evaporates under the sun, the salt deposit is left and harvested.

There is a huge variety of salts, from grey, coarse, Celtic, Himalayan pink, organic, fleur de sel to Hawaiian black and red salts. They all have their stories to tell. In England, sea salt from Maldon in Essex has deservedly become popular in the last decade among British cooks. In fact, salt has been gathered in that part of the country since Roman times. After high tides across the Mersea marshes, water is siphoned from the local river and processed to create a crystalline product with a gentle, tangy flavour and the texture of breadcrumbs.

Refined salt is more or less industrially extracted rock salt. This is mass-produced from naturally occurring salt deposits underground. It's normally sold as domestic table salt and, for no intelligible reason, is still what you mainly find in even the best restaurants. Avoid it. Apart from containing ugly anti-caking additives, it has no flavour and brings nothing to your cooking.

Some rock salts are sold unrefined and can have a more delicate impact than sea salt. All sorts of fabulous crystal rock salts come from the Himalayas and are highly prized by chefs around the world. They are said to be the purist, created in the mists of the mountains closest to heaven.

Used in cooking, perhaps surprisingly, salt has changing properties. The point at which you add it to your cooking can have different effects. And because water can vary in different parts of the world, the addition of salt will affect what you are cooking in different ways. If you live in an area with soft water (such as Scotland and some parts of Australia and North America), you should use plenty of salt when boiling green vegetables as it will help them maintain their colour. In areas of harder water, much less salt is needed. Vegetables and pulses with high cellulose content, such as carrots, squashes, potatoes, peas, lentils and beans, won't need much salt at all for cooking. Contrary to populist thought, adding salt does not lower the boiling point of water to any significant degree.

Some chefs say that you should only add salt after cooking, but in your kitchen there are only the rules that you make. You do whatever makes the food taste the way you like it.

Pepper

Like refined table salt, the proliferation of ground white pepper has reflected badly on this finest and most noble of spices. In medieval times, black pepper (piper nigrum) was the most common spice in cooking, but it has been suggested by historians that the rise of fine French cuisine in the seventeenth century led to a more gentle approach to seasoning.

There are four kinds of pepper: black, white, red and green, all of which come from the same plant but are harvested and produced differently. Each of them has a slightly different impact in cooking but it's no generalisation that your kitchen, and very many dishes, will be incomplete without at least a little freshly broken black pepper.

Because most pepper available in shops has already been ground or cracked by the time it is sealed and packaged and arrives in your kitchen, the interesting flavours and essential oils will have disappeared. This is one of the most important reasons for owning at least a pepper grinder but best of all a pestle and mortar. Exercise caution in what you purchase. Most of us have been exposed to those towering pepper phalluses brandished by cocky waiters in Italian trattorias, which never quite grind enough but demand huge energy to handle and are simply an embarrassment. Equally, most domestic versions succeed in grinding little more than powdered wood or plastic shavings on to the plate.

Be brave, get pounding. Smash open the little black devils in your mortar and catch a whiff of the pungency that emerges. Don't break them down too much; the more you do, the quicker the goodness disappears. But once you've got into the habit, you'll never want to use that tasteless white sneezing powder again. Serve pepper at the table in the mortar.

Have fun with the other peppercorns, too, particularly the red ones with game or strong-tasting meats that need an aromatic lift. Green pickled peppercorns are perfect with pasta or for an added bite with fish or chicken. You'll work it out.

A long-neglected Indonesian variety called Long Pepper (piper longum) has recently been rediscovered in kitchens. It's still hard to find but is worth searching out for its fiery, sweet, lingering over-taste. There are also tiny Madagascan peppercorns, which are hot and perky with an initial zing that makes them perfect for salads and fish. The green, dried Mexican peppercorn is, as you'd expect, full of gentle fire and works in a perfect flavour match with lime. There are many others from around the world with which you can experiment as you find them.

Lemons

Like oil, salt and pepper, lemons are simply indispensible in a kitchen. All too often they are undersold, making cameo appearances as skinny garnish slices in restaurants or wedged next to a bit of fish.

And yet these little orbs of concentrated sunshine possess properties without which any cook would be at a loss: aromatic oils from the zest to bring flavour, acidic citrus juices from the flesh to cut through fat and preserve freshness, and even fruit pectin in pith and seeds for the most adventurous to make jelly, marmalade and jam. Not forgetting, of course, among all those useful effects that life-giving

essence of robust health, vitamin C – in bucket-loads. Being ill without a lemony hot toddy with Scotch whisky is like being in love without Champagne.

Lemons are as important in cooking as salt. There is almost no dish which does not benefit from a squeeze of lemon. Very often you can use the juice instead of salt and it will draw out a different kind of flavour. When steaming vegetables such as leeks or carrots, the juice cauterises the delicate flavours, which might otherwise be lost through excessive exposure to heat. Cooking rice with half a lemon brushes off the starch and helps to stop the rice grains congealing. And lemon juice is the signature of most marinades, by neutralising fishy odours and tenderising meat. If you don't have a bottle of vinegar around, actually the juice of lemons and limes do perfectly well as a replacement in salad dressings and are ideal for mayonnaise.

But these are just a few of the things you can do with lemons. Just make sure you have plenty of them around. They can be handled roughly too. Slice one in half and squeeze it over your upturned palm, using your fingers to sieve out the pips. And when you are grating the zest, don't worry about being too picky. The pungency of those fragrant oils emerging from the skin will seduce any palate.

Preserved lemons are a mainstay in North African foods, particularly in Morocco where they put them in a jar with salt, leaving them for months, sometimes years, to soften and salinate, and thus making them the generous companions to poultry and fish tagines. They also work brilliantly with game, which usually has strong flavours that need to be subdued.

And when you've squeezed out the juice, before you throw away the empty peel, rub your hands with it. The oils and juice keep your skin smooth and they'll have that tantalising taste for your lover's delectation.

Garlic

There is a reason why your body may reek of garlic the morning after having a meal in some restaurants. It seems to exude relentlessly from the pores. No wonder Count Dracula hated it; the blood of all those virgins on his breath must have been bad enough without adding garlic to the mix.

For almost every food culture in the world, garlic is a significant part of cooking. But it really doesn't need to be overwhelming as it shares the behaviour of its close relatives, such as onions, leeks and chives, where the pungency when raw diverts to a gentle overlay of flavour when cooked.

Garlic is a more abused and violated ingredient than any other in the kitchen. It has become ubiquitous in highly over-processed forms in restaurants of all nationalities and decimated by the prevalence of the garlic 'crusher'. It is therefore, somewhat justifiably, hated by the culinary faint-hearted. But this is to do garlic an injustice. This noble bulb needs to be handled respectfully if you want to enjoy its matchless qualities.

If nothing else, garlic has healthy properties: its chemical compound helps to lower blood pressure, it is reputed to be anti-carcinogenic and anti-bacterial. Most importantly, it is entirely possible to eat garlic with no ill-effects on your breath or other people's olfactory senses.

It's simple. Garlic contains a sulphurous oil which gets into your blood. So the more you break it down prior to cooking – chopping it very fine or squeezing it through a press – the more that pungency courses straight into the bloodstream. Hence the powdered garlic deployed in many restaurants is just plain evil and has destroyed many hot dates and mornings after.

So here it is. Chop garlic into large pieces and toast it gently in oil before you add the other ingredients to any dish. You want it to be lightly browned, sweet and chewy. This approach will lend a gentle and discreet flavour, complementary and welcoming, with none of the throaty backbite. And it can course through the digestive system before it has time to saturate your circulation and bring any ill-effects to your breath.

There may be times when you want to give a strong wallop of garlic to something. Then you add it raw, usually before cooking, such as in a marinade or for something like a pesto sauce. But in those dishes, the time it needs to impart the strong flavours into the ingredients it accompanies, also tempers the whole, and if necessary you can remove it before eating.

Garlic can also be cooked completely whole without peeling, either in cloves or as a bulb. The latter is a delicacy in France but if you just want to add something special to a dinner, throw in some unpeeled cloves with the roasting potatoes and vegetables. There is no pleasure quite like squeezing out the sweet goo with your fingers.

Garlic can be eaten raw and can be pickled or marinated with olives, lemon and herbs. It can be rubbed on bread for the Italian staple *bruschetta* or the Mallorquin *pa amb oli*. Pesto genovese, tapenade and hummus all use raw garlic in the making and benefit from being left overnight to allow that powerful flavour to work its magic.

Bear in mind that this is a seasonal product and, unless you are buying it fresh, there has generally been a long time since it has been picked. So make sure the heads are firm and well covered in the papery skin and that there are no green shoots emerging, especially if you are buying a string. If you don't think you'll use it quickly, go for a couple of bulbs at a time. Always store garlic bulbs in a dry place, not in the fridge.

Like all the best ingredients, there are many varieties of garlic, in this case literally hundreds. Not so many of them hit the shelves of our local shops, but there are a few specialist growers and it's worth seeking them out. The nicest, most readily available garlic with the mottled purple skin is grown in the Auvergne. This rose garlic was the kind most favoured by 'Johnny Onions', the garlic sellers who travelled from France on the empty coal ships returning to Britain. This has a bite to it and it's worth getting a string in the winter to see you through. The other fairly accessible garlic delight is from Spain, called *rocambole*, with a deep, earthy flavour. There is also a giant 'elephant' garlic, which is quite fun for doing something a bit different but it is sweet and doesn't quite hold the same depth of flavour, so it's more like cooking with baby onions.

You'll see people fiddling unnecessarily, trying to peel garlic before chopping it. Be bold. Take the side of your knife blade (or anything flat and heavy) and use it to hit the garlic cloves lightly – just enough to crush them slightly. You can just nip off the end and they will easily slip out of their husk.

A note of caution: throw away the garlic crusher. They simply reduce the cloves to a pulpy, malodorous sludge that will infect your breath for days and add nothing to your cooking.

Using your Fridge

For those of us living in small urban flats, where space is at a premium, the fridge has become an oasis of cool, allowing us to keep things fresh. Even bigger homes rarely have larders and pantries, where different foodstuffs used to be safely stored at the right temperature to ensure they lasted. So these roomy cooling mechanisms with their attached freezers are incredibly useful to the cook. They allow one to keep a much wider selection of interesting produce at the ready for longer, which means that we can have more creative moments when suddenly faced with a hungry audience or a dish that needs pepping up.

Storing food in a fridge is an important way of keeping it safe. The cool temperature helps to keep the food fresh and slows the growth of most harmful microbes. At the same time, it does not change the characteristics of the food. Clearly the obvious things you want to keep in the fridge are the products you like to be cold and which last well because of that. So dairy products, meat, fish and some vegetables can be stored at just the right temperatures to keep them in the right state for as long as possible.

The proper temperature for the middle of a fridge is five degrees Celsius. However, the temperature is not constant throughout the interior and this means you can keep different sorts of foods at different temperatures. The coldest point in the fridge is the bottom shelf above the drawers, which is the best place to put fresh meat and fish. You should store dairy products, cooked meats and fish, leftovers and cakes higher up. The drawers at the bottom are warmer, or can be adjusted in posh fridges, and are therefore best for vegetables and fruits that can be damaged by lower temperatures. The compartments or shelves on the inside of the door are the warmest part of the refrigerator and, because the door is continually opening, they are the best place for jars, drinks and things that don't need a constant chill.

A big mistake is to fill the fridge too full. It's tempting as a cook to cram every section with leftovers and little morsels and titbits ready to extract at any given moment. But this is bad practice because if there is no space between the items, air cannot circulate, which is a vital part keeping things fresh and lowering the chance of microbes developing. Overloading will also encourage the accumulation of frost, which also prevents your fridge functioning efficiently.

Basically the minute fruit, vegetable, fish, beast or fowl is cut off from its life source, its cells stop reproducing and decomposition sets in more, or less, quickly. There are endless ways of making these products last longer and there's some fairly complex chemistry around the reasons why. Simply put, those with dense structures, which are less easily broken down – such as root vegetables or lean beef – can last for longer (days, weeks, even whole winters) than those that have very delicate flesh, such as fish, or that contain reactive sugary chemicals, such as soft summer fruits.

As with all things in the kitchen, you need to follow your intuition where keeping food fresh is concerned. Be led by your nose, which will always tell you if something is on the way out. We are mostly victims of a 'use-by' and 'sell-by' culture which has emerged with the rise of the supermarket and industrial food production. You need to be sensible about food at all times but there is no greater guide for that than your common sense.

It makes sense to use things up as quickly as necessary but a product saying on the label that it is out of date, doesn't mean it is. Millions of tonnes of food are thrown away needlessly every year in the UK, Europe and the US because of a slavish dependency on supermarket food safety policies. And these are only there to protect the producers from litigation. Decide for yourself if a pint of milk is on the turn or if a chicken can last an extra day or two; more often than not, products will last much longer than they say on the label. A useful rule of thumb is that simple products with no additives, for example a hard cheese, an open tin of anchovies or bag of fresh herbs, will last much longer than processed foods that rely on stabilising chemicals, such as a tub of processed hummus or cottage cheese.

Other than the obvious things everyone is likely to have in a fridge, there are many extras which will bring joy to any kitchen. Mustard of all varieties tends to last better if kept a little cool. Unless you like to make your own English mustard from powder, then having a tube or jar of it is useful, alongside a less aggressive variety such as Dijon, for a gentler touch. Tomato purée, horseradish sauce, capers, cornichons, anchovies, branded mayonnaise, ketchup, pesto and pickles all survive happily in the fridge door, which also makes for swift access.

Another useful addition is a jar of breadcrumbs, which seem to last indefinitely. Every time you have a stale loaf, slice it up, pop into a moderate oven and allow to toast completely, then grind it in the food processor, leave it to cool completely and store the crumbs in a jar. Then you'll always have them at the ready for dipping with egg for coating goujons, frying aubergines or padding out a chicken liver pâté. Tossing breadcrumbs into par-boiled potatoes before roasting will add an extra crunch.

Most of all, you need to use your fridge like an advanced cupboard where you can store things you don't want to use up immediately. It will become like a little emporium which, when you feel like cooking, you can visit to find some delightful ingredients to toss up a salad or decant some stock for a risotto.

Most fridges these days come with advanced freezers attached. There is lots more to learn about what to keep there in terms of produce, but this is a huge advantage for cooks who like to make large batches of food such as soups and stews to stash away for a hard winter or to keep a spouse well fed in your absence. You can freeze fresh green herbs such as chopped coriander and parsley, keeping them in bags to fish out for adding to a dish at the last minute.

Look after your fridge, keep it clean at all times, don't allow nasty bugs to lurk in its nooks and crannies and it will be a faithful servant.

Stocking the Cupboards

Since time immemorial, humans have been finding ways to preserve the abundance of harvest-time through the cold or lean months, when the riches of the earth are less plentiful. Even today, the ancient processes of drying, curing and salting are still prevalent all over the world. From the dried game (*biltong*) of the *voortrekkers* to salt cod (*bacalao*) from Spain, there have always been ways of maintaining the availability of vital nutritious foods which would otherwise decay.

Preserving and pickling were traditionally perennial domestic enterprises from country houses to humble cottages, where cookers and tables groaned with preserving pans and jars, seeds, spices and vinegars ready to pack into the cupboards for the winter. Industrialisation increased production of these delicacies, eventually making it easier than ever to stock up with all the necessaries for your kitchen, to steady you whenever the need arises.

Jars of pickles and conserves are essential stock for the kitchen. Life wouldn't be complete without a fine vintage marmalade or some pickled walnuts winking down from the kitchen shelf. But the days are long gone when we have pantries full of bottled and preserved foods.

You'll have your own favourite titbits. If you can imagine yourself unscrewing the lid and poking a finger in to fish out a mouthful of something mouth-watering, then just make sure it's in the kitchen.

The development of the canning industry is said to have been inspired by Napoleon Bonaparte. He set up a competition to find a way of preserving the food he needed to keep his troops alive through the privations of long and difficult campaigns. The prize was awarded to a chef called Nicholas Appert, who realised that food would last by first heating it, thus killing any festering bacteria, and then sealing it in an airtight container, keeping the food in a vacuum. Appert's invention used glass bottles sealed with wax. Soon after, in Britain, the first patent was granted for a process where food was sealed in durable tin cans. This technical development became the edible mainstay of exploration, colonisation and wars during the Victorian era.

There is a certain snobbishness over fresh food compared to what we now call tinned food, and it is generally on the lower shelf in perceptions of quality. But for the competent cook, some tins are a godsend. Like everything else, if you look for quality, you'll find it. Indeed, arguably many of the core ingredients you need to have in the kitchen are better in tins than fresh. The reason is simple. Often the journey to the factory and the tin is shorter than the journey to supermarket shelves in far-off countries. So the food is fresher when it is tinned and the nutrient levels are higher. Not to mention the environmental benefits of sea transportation over the energy used for air freighting fresh produce for thousands of miles across the globe.

Pulses and beans, which provide essential protein and are excellent for maintaining a healthy balanced diet, are perfectly suited to being in tins. The fibre is good for our digestive systems and has beneficial side effects, such as reducing cholesterol and thus the risk of heart disease. In tins, they tend towards being more juicy and moist than their dried cousins. Of course, many will argue with this, but the kitchen is the home of pragmatics not purism.

You can, of course, buy many different dried beans and pulses, but some can take a long time to soak before cooking. So if time is an issue, instead opt for quality tinned varieties with no additives and you will succeed every time.

There are any number of suggestible tins and jars for you to have in the kitchen cupboard or fridge, which will enable you to whisk up some of the standard dishes we talk about in later chapters.

But don't forget eating should be fun. Like most activities in life, it can become humdrum. Ensure that you stock a few of life's little luxuries. A tin of *confit de canard*, lobster bisque or beef consommé will nourish you through any financial, emotional or health crisis.

Pulses and Grains

Pulses are essentially the seeds from plants called legumes. Despite their modern association with vegetarians, we have, in fact, been eating them since at least 6000BC.

Everywhere in the world has its own varieties of bean, so you need to experiment to find the ones you most like to cook with. In the UK, we are most familiar with the ubiquitous and redoubtable haricot bean, a variety of which is used for canned baked beans, and the kidney bean, most commonly found in chilli con carne. But there are many more interesting ones to try, and each cooks and complements in slightly different ways: haricots, borlotti, butter, cannellini, flageolet, Greek gigandes and Spanish faba.

There are three main varieties of lentils: brown, green (puy) and red.

The green ones, puy lentils or *lentilles vertes*, originally come from France and are the finest, with the most robust flavour and consistency. Unlike beans, which tend to need soaking overnight and can take a long time to cook, dried lentils are easily cooked, though there are some highly acceptable tinned offerings.

If you are a fan of hummus, which can be made in minutes, a tin of white chickpeas is an important item to stock. And they are definitely a staple if you get adventurous with cooking dishes from the Indian sub-continent.

Vegetables

Try to avoid canned vegetables where their fresh or frozen counterpart is better. Green vegetables lose their colour and some of their essential vitamin content in the process. Tinning things like potatoes and mushrooms is just silly and unnecessary. If you like sweetcorn, best of luck to you, but it makes a vulgar show on a plate.

On the other hand, the quality canned Italian plum tomato retains a richness hard to find in most intensively farmed fresh tomatoes. When picked, plum tomatoes have less of the pulp than normal varieties of tomato and are easily seeded and skinned. They also retain more of the highly beneficial antioxidant lycopene. Other vegetables that are tasty from cans or jars include peppers, globe artichoke hearts and white asparagus but remember to check the label before you buy to make sure they are free from the tedious preservatives used by mass producers. Any of these can be quickly chopped into a salad or added to a risotto.

Things in jars are much more of a subjective and selective question. It is more or less entirely based on what tastes your palate leans towards. Capers provide a flavour boost for lots of dishes and you can buy them in different forms. Their delicate floral punch is the perfect splash of individuality you sometimes require to stand out in a dish. They come jarred, salted or in brine. There is also a bigger relative called caperberries which can be sliced or popped into a salad whole. Sun-dried tomatoes are also an asset in the cupboard. You can buy them in oil or dried so all you have to do is soak them in water. Their intense, focused flavour has a meaty bite to it.

It's quite delightful at times to be able to fish out a pickled onion or jalapeño to tantalise the appetite before dinner or accompany some cold meat and cheese. There are myriad varieties to choose from. Whether you are shopping in the hypermarket or a farm shop, go for something that has no colouring or flavour enhancers and that looks from the outside of the jar that you'd like to eat it. Something which looks as though it escaped from the shrunken heads department of an ancient museum or medical institute is not to be encouraged.

Fish

Fish tin well. And because it is mostly the smaller varieties, the bones are softened and the calcium and many of the essential fishy oils we need in our diet are preserved. A tin of pilchards or sardines served on wholemeal toast is one of the most complete and beneficial meals you can have (notwithstanding the propensity of oily fish returning on the breath at inopportune moments!)

In the UK, ninety per cent of cupboards are host to a tin of tuna. There are a few different varieties available, for example blue and yellow fin, albacore and skipjack. Some have more or less dark meat, and they are variously preserved in oil, brine or fresh water. Most tinned tuna is skipjack but albacore, with its whiter meat, is also fairly readily available.

Be aware that tinned tuna doesn't count as an oily fish because most of the Omega 3 disappears when it is cooked before tinning. But it is still a versatile ingredient and a healthy source of protein. However, salmon, sardines, mackerel, trout and pilchards all retain their oily fish status in tins. They can be judiciously mixed with other ingredients and, under the right influences, provide excellent sustenance.

When dealing with fish today, all cooks need to understand the meaning of sustainability. Across the world, the oceans are seeing dramatic falls in the stocks of our favourite wild fish, and if we don't halt that process, like many other species of fish, tuna could be close to extinction, as could many other species.

You'll read more and more about the Marine Stewardship Council (MSC) in the coming years. If you love fish on your plate, you'll want to keep it in the sea. This means breaking the habits of eating the fish species that are under threat and trying new things instead. That's what the MSC helps us do. The first MSC-approved tinned tuna was launched in 2009. Find it and buy it.

It is hard to imagine what a clever cook would do without anchovies. These silvery fry are so versatile. But much maligned for their trashy cameo appearances on cheap pizzas, they've got a bad name. Even if you find them too strong on their own, they are a cook's mainstay and you should always have a jar of them in the fridge to impart that tiny sliver of flavour that will lend itself to almost anything it is cooking with. They can bring the pizzazz to a Caesar dressing and a rich, sweetness to roast lamb without imparting any fishiness. When you are buying anchovies, look for quality. Italian is best. They are initially cured in brine – which causes the strength in their flavour – and then tinned in good olive oil. Like all tinned fish, it's best to buy the brands that don't make unwanted additions of herbs or garlic. You always want to be able to do your own flavouring; it so often depends on your mood.

Fruit

Tinned fruits are not bad for you; nor are they better than the real thing. But sometimes, they are just easier. And they do retain some of their nutrients, which long-travelled fresh fruits may have lost. As usual, go for the brands where there are no additives and the fruit is in juice rather than syrup.

It's useful to have a tin of morello cherries handy as they are perfect companions for duck or game but, as you'll learn with all shopping, it's the same as looking for clothes: first you see something you like and then you work out what you'll wear it with.

Dried fruits can be a godsend in replacing high sugar content foods and are an excellent way of fuelling an energy boost in the long, low hours of the afternoon. And just sometimes you may want to employ them in a savoury dish such as a tagine or in an impromptu pudding.

You'll certainly want marmalade and preserves. If you are buying them, again go for quality. The thing you have to watch is the sugar to fruit quotient. You are looking for something with sixty per cent fruit content, which is harder than you might think. If you make your own, you'll find they are not simple, but they can be fun moments in the kitchen calendar.

The Carbs

We have a dysfunctional relationship with the kinds of important ballast we need to survive. And carbohydrates have got a bad name. Bread, pasta, rice and noodles (which are largely the same thing) have become the enemy of the muscled, skinny generation, yet we can benefit so much from what they give us, even if we do want to get fit and healthy. And it's certain that in every food culture across the world, some form of grain-based carbohydrate does form a significant element of cooking.

Starches are naturally occurring carbohydrates. As omnivores, the ability to digest starchy foods has been thought to have been an essential element in our evolution. Enzymes in our saliva and pancreas break down starch into the important sugars that we need for energy.

Many of our favourite foods contain carbohydrates, but they tend to be indigestible before cooking: potatoes, wheat and rice being the most obvious examples One way to make starches digestible is to expose them to heat. So we boil them. When they cook, the heat and liquid start permeating the surface and they start breaking down.

Eaten with caution and cooked simply, carbs provide an invaluable balance to a healthy diet. And why not? No supper can be better than a simple pesto pasta or asparagus risotto. Life could never truly be complete without the occasional sustaining bowl of rice pudding and jam. How joyless life would be without *brie de meaux* and a Parisian baguette.

Of course, we have to be careful. A life full of pies and baked pastas will soon have you leaping up the Body Fat Index, but treated with respect and seen as individual ingredients, these dried foods work. For a start, in cold countries we need the energy that the starch and sugars from carbs give us. And, more importantly for the newly trained kitchen devil, rice, pasta and noodles offer some perfect opportunities for quick wins in the cooking stakes. With already interesting shapes and textures, the right amount of cooking and a minimal influx of other ingredients can transform a basic dish into something spectacular.

Rice and Other Grains

Rice is the grains of a species of grass called *oryza sativa* and is the sustaining force behind a huge percentage of the world's population. There are many thousands of varieties of this species but we only need to think about cooking a few of them. They include long, medium and short grain and wild rice. The two you certainly want to have in your kitchen are a long grain, and a medium grain for risotto. Pudding rice is a short grain. Long-grain rice, such as Basmati, cooks to a fluffy consistency, where the grains remain separate. And short-grain or medium-grain rice, such as Arborio risotto rice, becomes more sticky when cooked, which makes it the best for risottos.

The other grains you are most likely to come across as you begin your adventures in cooking are pearl barley, polenta, bulgur and buckwheat and a strange Andean crop called quinoa. Each of them comes from a different plant and requires slightly different handling. When making a stew or soup, pearl barley will bring you some bulk, and as the gluten is released it adds that essential gloopy quality to your mess of potage. It's for the same reason that barley was used to create a substantial, smooth fruit cordial called lemon barley water.

It's made simply by pouring boiling water on sugar, barley and lemons, straining, then chilling.

Polenta inhabits a world of its own today in Italian cooking. It's made from ground maize and is frankly rather bland, being the progenitor of that miserable slop which was the fuel of earlier centuries and civilisations, called gruel. And if it isn't prepared expertly, it has the characteristics of a quick-setting wall filler.

Bulgur and buckwheat, however, are rewarding and enormously healthy ingredients to work with. You boil them in water, as you do pasta, and they make for perfect, healthy salads. Because they are essentially tasteless, you need to use the Middle Eastern dish *tabouleh*, as your exemplar. With lots of fresh herbs, olive oil, lemon and seasonings and the addition of finely chopped raw vegetables, you can create the perfect lasting, lunchtime sustenance.

Quinoa (pronounced *keenwa*) actually comes from a bush that grows high up in the Andean pastures. It was revered as an ingredient by the ill-fated Incas and its harvesting was proscribed by the invading Spanish colonists, for whom it represented a subversive foodstuff, having a part in some spiritual ceremonies. Worldwide consumption has really only increased relatively recently through health shops. You need to soak off the husks of the grains before cooking, as they can be pretty hard to digest.

Pasta and Noodles

Pastas, couscous and noodles are also grain-based carbs. Pasta is made from ground durum wheat. It has a high starch content which hardens as the pasta mixture is dried, almost like glue. When it is boiled again, the starch compounds soften. Its versatility is similar to rice and it appears in different forms, from semolina to couscous, particularly in lots of Middle Eastern and North African cooking.

For pasta, the flour is ground very fine and mixed with water, shaped and dried into shapes, as with the commonly found pastas, for example spaghetti, linguine, penne and fusilli. There are hundreds of different colours, shapes and sizes of pasta, which tend to relate to the specific villages in which they are made. It's an enjoyable adventure to find your favourites.

Pasta can also be made with egg, stuffed with various ingredients, as in ravioli or tortellini, and dried. It is sold in supermarkets in both dried and also 'fresh' versions, but the received view is that there is no advantage to buying 'fresh'. Either eat it on the day it is made, at home or from an Italian deli, or cook it from dried.

Noodles work pretty much like pasta, having an amazing number of shapes and sizes, depending on use and where they are made. Some are created from ingredients other than wheat flour, such as peas, mung beans, rice and even, in Korea, from acorns. You choose the ones you like most.

Nuts and Seeds

Nuts and seeds are little concentrated earthly nuggets of protein. All the efforts of whatever plant or tree they come from have gone into making these offspring on which their future depends. Actually what distinguishes a nut from a seed is one of those biological questions which, as cooks, we simply gloss over. We simplistically refer to the big ones with hard shells as nuts and the little versions without shells as seeds. Which will do for us, as the kitchen is no place for botanical pedantry.

Fortunately, Mother Nature has taught us to be sufficiently wise to

learn how to harvest this precious commodity without damaging the cycle of life, and so we have an amazing variety of nuts and seeds to use in our cooking. The real benefit of using them is that they contain rich natural oils and are full of beneficial energy compounds.

The nuts we most commonly use in cooking are pine nuts (really seeds), walnuts, almonds, chestnuts, cashews and pistachios. When you lightly toast the first two varieties, they add generous flavour to vegetable dishes, pasta or salads. But you have to watch them like a hawk as they turn to cinders in seconds. The heat allows the oils and some extra flavours to emerge from the nut, though the pay-off is that some of the vitamin goodness is then lost. Apparently the chemicals that form at high temperatures in nuts can also contribute to ageing. But you'd have to be eating an awful lot of nuts for that to happen.

Cashews or pistachios are ideal to give bite to stir-fries, but it's worth smashing them up a bit first, otherwise they can be a bit of a mouthful. Almonds are best bought whole with their skins, which are easily removed if you soak them in boiling water. They can also be added to a dish that needs some extra crunch, like a fish pie or kedgeree, and some baking dishes call for ground almonds rather than flour. When the time of year comes round for chestnuts roasting on the fire, be careful to prick the skins first, particularly if you're actually doing them in the oven, otherwise they'll explode and take a lot of cleaning up. A tin of chestnut purée is always a handy staple for the cupboard and makes a beguiling ice-cream when mixed with honey or chocolate. It's also an autumnal, nutty addition to a game soup.

Some seeds, such as caraway, fennel, cumin, nigella and cardamom, appear in the culinary periodic table as spices. But other seeds have their uses in all the same ways as nuts, although probably need to make selective appearances, except in lighter dishes where they won't get lost, such as salads or stir-fries. Among these are pumpkin, sunflower, poppy and sesame seeds, which all have something to add and, like nuts, are bagged full of goodness. Flax and linseeds have a reputation for helping digestive problems, though the husks can be an irritation, so if you are suffering from a digestive disorder, grind them in your food processor and spoon them into dishes as a powder. It will certainly keep things moving in the right direction.

Seasonings and Condiments

Even the best cooks can't bring life to every dish without help from seasonings. And although there is little that can't be achieved by the big five – oil, salt, pepper, lemons and garlic – one of the things you will do as your capacity to cook grows is to acquire a selection of jars and bottles, serried small and tall, ready to season at a second's notice. There are no hard-and-fast rules here, you must work with the palette of your own choosing. But exercise caution: there is nothing more useless than shelves full of things you buy and never use.

The best advice is to find your favourites and become confident in

their use. In Greece, for example, the monks of Mount Athos have long been known for their quiet, austere lifestyle. These hirsute ascetics have lived here since 923AD. It is a simple existence which has changed little since. But they have been shown to have extraordinarily long lives and low levels of disease thanks to their diet. They season their home-grown produce with a few uncomplicated flavours: lemon, cumin, pepper and oregano. And they seldom stray from this combination.

Presented with the vast array of herbs and spices available in dried form, it's almost impossible to know what to buy. Most households around the country have jars of tasteless spices and herbs, like ranks of toy soldiers long-forgotten in the attic. Any flavour they ever had has long since faded. And they are only occasionally revived with wistful looks and a snatch of nostalgia.

Don't fall into the trap of collecting these hapless weeds. For a start, very few dried herbs retain a strong enough flavour to be useful in cooking. Those that dry reasonably well – such as rosemary, bay, oregano (marjoram) and thyme – are not improved by the process and in this form can easily overpower your cooking without bringing any real benefit. Drying other herbs – such as mint, tarragon and basil – actually changes the flavour they impart, and not for the better. Although they might look nice hanging up, if you like the Tuscan kitchen look.

Always employ fresh herbs, if you can, for the richest colours, tastes and smells. If you are going to use dried herbs, you will get the best performance from a concoction called *herbes de provence*, which contains all of the above. But use it only sparingly in and emergency, when rescuing something that might otherwise be lost.

Spices, on the other hand, are a different matter and it takes a really specialist knowledge of the dishes you are cooking to know how to use them well. Along with gold and silk, spices were the first general commodity of luxury trade across the world and are the stuff of legend. They seem to evoke the heady, swarming pungency of the grand cities of the East. From North Africa to China, map-making and navigation were driven by the commerce of the ancient spice routes; wars were waged and empires built on their almost mythic properties.

Spices can either be powerful allies or humiliating enemies, so immerse yourself slowly in their world. Where fresh herbs bring something verdant, fragrant and brightening, spices can completely transform with their complex perfumes and rich, edgy flavours. Understanding the magic of spices is a mighty talent. And one which can take many years of practice to really understand.

Choosing spices is like deciding what perfume to wear. Keep it simple. Spices give a clear signal of their potential from the outset. You want a sensational smell, colour or taste that will linger. The best way is to start as a novice and acquire a small and adequate collection. And the best place to do that is in one of the souks of Morocco. But if you aren't able to travel, find a shop or market near you and ask their advice. You might start with: a whole nutmeg for grating; cumin and fennel seeds, which can be ground in your mortar; sweet ground cinnamon and ginger to bring exotic qualities to vegetable dishes, and of course rice or bread and butter puddings, or ice-cream. The most important point here is to use them in decent quantities so that you taste them as their properties enrich your food and body. As you become confident with their use, add turmeric root, nigella seeds, paprika and the stirring *ras el hanout*, a mix of many spices like *garam masala*, another must for the spice enthusiast, for making curries.

Spices lose their potency. So if you have a cupboard full of jars of branded spices and you can't remember when or where you bought them, they will probably have been there too long. Throw them out and start again. There is something charming about seeing the old women of North Africa or Turkey shopping for a tiny paper of spices to use in the lunch dish they are just about cook.

Adding Flavour

The term condiment used to be confined to salt, pepper, vinegar and mustard. Many tasteless and unsightly 'condiment sets' still linger on dining room tables to remind us of this. However, in today's kitchen, the term covers a whole range of saucy balms and emollients. These can be essential delights which bring flavour to the table.

First up, a vinegar or two. Don't complicate matters unnecessarily. In the early stages you might want to try a red or white wine vinegar to use for salad dressings. But it's powerful stuff and lemon or lime juice will often make a useful replacement. There is no reason to use anything other than that freshly squeezed from the fruit.

Vinegar is a solution of fermented wine, cider or sherry and is known to have medicinal properties. The Roman legionnaires who, after all, managed to take over most of the known world, drank it with water. Then, like now, it was thought to have healing properties. Drink it with a little honey to stimulate your internal organs or pique your immune system into action.

There is one vinegar, which has become massively popular in the last decade or two, called balsamic vinegar. This has been made in or around the town of Modena in Italy since the Middle Ages. It is not strictly speaking a vinegar, as it is not made from alcohol but from freshly pressed Trebbiano grape juice. This is boiled down to the consistency of syrup and then put into open oak casks to ferment. It then undergoes a process of evaporation and concentration over a period of ten years until it is finally poured into a juniper cask, where it is 'finished'.

Only a few thousand litres of authentic balsamic vinegar are produced each year. So most of what you buy cheaply is not the real thing and is industrially produced. Avoid that and go for something special. It is an ally in the kitchen and can be sprinkled on to anything before or after cooking to spruce it up. Like the best wines, you don't always want to drink one. But you want to know that there's one in the rack.

Soy sauce is the samurai of ingredients in your cupboard. It can charge out and wrest flavour from even the most insipid plate of food. Somehow it draws out what's there and injects something of its own. It's common all over South-East Asia, where it has become a basic condiment. It is made from fermented soya beans, roasted barley or wheat and salt mixed with water. Sometimes there are additions to the mix, such as fish sauce, mushroom and even pork, to create different strength and depth. The whole is allowed to age and then bottled.

Soy sauce has so much flavour thanks to the much maligned compound monosodium glutamate, widely known as MSG. Contrary to public ignorance about such things, MSG is not necessarily bad for you. It is a naturally occurring substance which was only identified in seaweed by the Japanese company Ajinomoto in 1907. The name it was given, *umame*, actually translates as 'deliciousness'. Like one of those other kitchen friends (I might mention Marmite, Bovril, Parmesan cheese, bouillon mix and other loyal seasonings), you know you can invite soy sauce to any occasion to fill an unexpected space. Have some around.

Working with Ingredients

While learning to cook is a journey, there is no set route. But as with all interesting journeys, you need to know the means by which you are going to get there. This is why it's so important for you to go it alone. Starting with recipes may seem easier, but they won't necessarily teach you anything, so you're effectively learning to cook by numbers. And the problem is that you will become reliant on someone else's imagination, always having to keep up with their culinary journeys rather than enjoying your own. Cooking this way is the difference between package holidays and being well travelled. Nonetheless, like the best guide books, a shelf full of inspirational cookbooks makes for wonderful reading, a useful resource and a reliable reference. But they won't actually teach you to be a cook.

The first step of your journey is actually to want to cook something. It may seem a bit obvious but this needs to be based not on necessity but a relish for the unknown. The second step is the belief that you can, a willingness to jump in and have a go. Next you just need to learn some simple rules about preparing and cooking. Then, as your confidence grows, you can become as creative as you like. You'll soon find the energy and enthusiasm to take risks, try new things and cook them in different ways. Starting with some basic dos and don'ts will set you on course. So the adventure begins.

By now, you should have a kitchen stocked with the ingredients you like and the right tools at hand. When deciding what you are going to cook, it helps to start with something simple that you already like. If roast chicken, cottage pie or game soup are your favourite, begin with them. By learning this way, even if it goes wrong, at least you will know how it should have ended up.

You need to select your ingredients and then you have to prepare them for cooking. To do this, you have to work out what qualities they already have and what they need from you. So first off, touch your food. Hold it. Only feeling it with your hands will tell you what to do with it. This carnal knowledge of what you eat is one of the keys to unlocking the secrets of cooking. Is it firm or fleshy, rough or smooth, long or round, clean or dirty, dressed or undressed? Can it be taken in hand; does it need to be beaten? Can you leave it to fester or will it sulk? Will it perk up or become self-centred when introduced to different companions?

Grasping a dead bird, chopping a carrot, knowing which bits of a fish to remove, just holding something the right way to cut into it or reshape it, brings you closer to the delight of eating it. By handling food, we quickly learn when it is best to wash, scrub, peel, chop, slice, fillet, marinate or just leave well alone.

These questions can only really be answered by experience. But asking them from the outset will send you in the right direction. Getting physical with your food soon produces results.

Knife Skills

One of the most important lessons in cooking is learning how to use your weapon. A knife is your best friend in the kitchen. But it's also a potentially lethal enemy, so it's important to know how to use it properly. If you have acquired a suitable cook's knife with a wide blade and strong handle, now you need to practise holding it properly.

Pretend to make a pistol with your hand, with your index finger and thumb at 90 degrees and your other three fingers around the grip. Place the knife in the palm of your hand in this shape. Pinch the end of the blade between thumb and index finger and let the knife nestle in your hand. It should feel light but firm, an extension of your arm, like a tennis racquet.

When slicing or chopping, the way you use your other hand is equally important. You must never hold your fingers out as if supporting a snooker cue, always have them gripping what you are cutting, like a claw, with the fingers turned in so that the side of the blade uses the flat of the middle section of the fingers as its guide.

If you have bought a quality chef's knife, the blade of the knife is wide and slightly bowed, like the keel of a boat. It is like this so that you can keep the blade on the surface of the board while chopping and slicing. As you cut, the blade should slide gently forward and back and slice as the other hand guides. Whatever knife you are using, always cut away from you and try to build up a safe rhythm. I recommend asking a friendly chef to show you how to do it properly because it will make a huge difference to the agility and speed with which you handle your ingredients. This skill requires lots of practice, but with that practice, you'll certainly find it gets easier.

A note of caution: don't use a chef's knife after you have started on the bottle. This is such a dangerous instrument and when you're inebriated it's as risky as driving a car. Your hands may bear many scars of over-enthusiastic knife-wielding as you're preparing dinner parties, and hospitals see more emergencies from domestic kitchens on Christmas Day than any other.

You may want to learn to use other sorts of knife, such as the filleting and paring varieties. There are lots available but they will require some manual agility too. My advice before moving on, is to stick with one until you feel completely confident you could show someone else how to use it.

Preparing Vegetables

Even today, overcooked, tedious and predictable vegetables remain the curse of many a table. Despite the efforts that many cooks make to create interesting main dishes, they often fail to attend to the natural brilliance of vegetables. Sweaty, overcooked cabbage, pale, mushy broccoli and tasteless carrots still make unwanted, all too regular appearances. This is unnecessary. Not only should vegetables on their own present the most enticing possibilities for a cook but even the usual suspects can be reinvented with attentiveness and imagination.

Vegetables are the perfect playground for the apprentice cook. They present so many options for cutting, slicing, shredding and cooking whole. The important thing is not to drown them or over-expose them to heat, which dilutes their flavours and nutrient value. (If it does all go wrong, you can always turn them into soup.) To start with just go out there and buy some vegetables that you like the look of. And be bold with your choices. You learn to cook a pumpkin by having a go, not reading a book.

Vegetables are often muddy, have skin, stalks, husks, pods or roots. So handle them and have a look all round them before deciding how to prepare them for cooking. For a start, if they are fresh from the garden where mud, bugs, slugs or disease might have had a go at them, give them a wash before you start. Leave them in your big colander to dry off or cover it with a cloth, turn it upside down and shake out the water.

Don't leave vegetables soaking for too long in water. If you are stepping out for a stroll or a snifter in the pub before embarking on a Sunday lunch, then don't leave them for more than a couple of hours. If you do soak them, it is not clear whether adding salt makes any difference.

For any salad leaves, such as spinach, greens, lettuce or rocket, once you've washed them you want to get the liquid off quickly so they don't become waterlogged. The same colander method will work, or a plastic spinner gets them really dry after washing. But do make sure you have expunged any stray bugs before doing so; they have a habit of hanging on even if the spinning makes them dizzy.

For heavier leaves that you are going to cook, such as spring greens, chard or kale, you can fish them straight from the sink to the pot, as you need to add a little extra water when you start cooking them anyway. Incidentally, these leaves can also be frozen easily, after softening for a few minutes in boiling water, called blanching.

Deciding how you cut vegetables will depend on what you are serving them with and how you like eating them. Food fashions have changed over the years. Carrots were always sliced in rounds until in the 1980s chefs universally discovered the sophisticated delights of carrots *julienne*, cut like batons. It doesn't really matter how you cut anything but the shorter the cooking time for most vegetables, the more of their essential goodness they maintain. So if you want them to cook quickly, chop them thinner and steam or stir-fry them.

One of the best uses for a microwave oven is for cooking green vegetables that quickly spoil, for example asparagus, mangetout, broccoli and green beans. Just put them in a container with a few centimetres of water, cover and microwave for a minute or two. It's pretty much the same thing as steaming but simpler. As a rule of thumb, it's always better to undercook vegetables; they will taste better and everyone will feel healthy.

Other vegetables do respond better to being cooked whole or roughly chopped and, of course, if you are adding vegetables to a slow cooking stew, they will both absorb and lend more flavour if you leave them in larger pieces. Whatever the outcome you're looking for, always cut away any of the tough, woody bits: cores, stalks or husks.

You'll work out your own preferred ways of cooking, but here are a few tips for preparing and cooking some of our most commonplace vegetables.

Root Vegetables

Purists will say that vegetables shouldn't be peeled because the strongest nutrient content is in the skin. This is unproven, though keeping the skin will preserve some of the nutrients inside vegetables during cooking and certainly gives some fibre, which helps digestion. When root vegetables, such as potatoes, turnips and carrots, are fresh from the ground, their skin is soft, so just a scrub or a wash is fine. But if they are old season, you'll probably want to peel them. For my money, the tough skin of large turnips or swedes always need to be peeled.

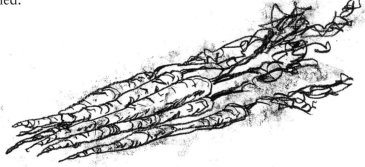

If you want tasty carrots, don't boil them; sauté them raw in oil or butter for a bit, then when they begin to soften, add a little water and let it boil off.

Celeriac has re-emerged as a classic winter root vegetable which, when peeled, can be roasted as chips, puréed or chopped into stews.

Salsify makes rare appearances but has a soft intensity grated into salads or blended with a beef consommé to a cold soup.

Turnips and swedes are both mustardy roots which work well almost any way – sautéed, mashed or roasted – and are perfect additions to stews and casseroles.

Potatoes

By reputation, the potato, 'tattie' or 'spud' is the mainstay of British cooking. And who wouldn't need the sturdy carbohydrate support they give our diet in such inclement weather. Unusually, they are hard to get wrong, whether mashed, roasted, baked or nicely boiled with a knob of butter and some parsley. But they are an example of the kind of vegetable that you need to get to know how to cook. Fortunately, most potatoes bought in supermarkets have guidelines on the packaging as to how they are best deployed. But if not, it's easy to work it out. You hear them referred to as waxy or floury, which represents how much moisture to fibre content there is. It's all to do with the season the tubers are planted and their growing patterns.

What you need to know is that a waxy potato is wetter and too gluey for mashing and a floury one is drier and therefore less good in salads. You'll learn which is which but if you are unsure which type you have, put a spoonful of salt in a glass jug and fill it with water.

When dropped into the water, a floury spud will almost always sink to the bottom, while a waxy one should float. New potatoes, which are small, are pretty versatile, though it might be a waste to mash them. Big potatoes can be cut to whatever size you want, though they might not have the delicacy of taste you need for a salad.

Again, the jury is out where the skin is concerned. You may want to keep the skins if you're baking them, but when they are knobbly and scarred it's best to strip them naked. You'll often find new potatoes, for example Jersey Royals, with that raggedy paper skin. Just give them a rub with your hands in water, boil and serve with butter.

Onions, Shallots and Leeks

These are all members of the *Alium* family. When raw, they are hard for the stomach to digest, bad for the breath and the sulphury compounds they release make your eyes water. There is very little reason ever to serve them uncooked (apart perhaps from incredibly finely chopped into steak tartare or potato salad) unless you have a bizarre palate and like the overweening choke of sulphur. Spring onions and Spanish onions are a little sweeter and more palatable, and require very little cooking.

All onions, when softened in oil or butter, develop a characteristic sweetness which intensifies to caramel the more they are cooked, which makes them the perfect basis for so many dishes. You can do almost anything with an onion or shallot, including just baking it whole in its skin.

Leeks produce a natural thickening agent or 'mucilage' (from carbohydrates and protein), which is useful if you are making stocks and stews. But don't overcook them if you're serving them as an accompaniment as this makes them slimy and rather bland.

Beans

With the kinds of fresh beans you eat whole, such as French or runner beans, as you take off the end stalks, draw them back along the pod, removing any chewy strings. Do the same along the other side. If they are tough, do it with a paring knife.

Broad beans are the hero of the family, having an almost unrivalled versatility. When young, they are sweet and profoundly generous in flavour. As they get older, you should take some of the skins away, which can be quite bitter. After cooking, just squeeze the edge of the bean with thumb and forefinger and the pert, green treasure will emerge.

Peas

The secret is now out that frozen peas beat everything but those you have just shelled from your own garden or pinched from a local farmer. The pea harvester is a behemoth, which trundles slowly across the fields, wrapping up the whole process in minutes, so they are quickly frozen, young and sweet.

Mangetout and sugar snap peas are varying forms of immature peas and can be eaten whole. Be warned, they are easily overcooked and should be added to any hot dish at the last minute before being served. You want them to lend the greenest colour to your plate. Nothing is less appetising than something young, looking old before its time.

Brassicas

These are all members of the amazingly prolific mustard family and include broccoli, spinach, cabbage, cauliflower, Brussels sprouts, kale, collard greens, *pak choi* and kohlrabi. They are full of health-giving properties. Just cut out the stalky bits and, as with all green vegetables, don't overcook them. We all remember from school dinners, and perhaps today some of the less upmarket hotel chains, the flaps of sodden cabbage and mushy broccoli. This is completely unnecessary and comes from over-cooking. All of these vegetables respond well to steaming or quickly stir-frying, which leaves them green and with a crunch.

Red cabbage is very popular in Northern Europe and China and turns a royal blue when cooked. Unusually, this variety doesn't mind slowly stewing, sometimes with the addition of something sweet such as apples or raisins.

Tomatoes

Woefully, this fine fruit has been so over-produced that it has become a largely tasteless addition to most dishes. Even in the British fry-up, tomatoes are usually served watery, raw and cold. This is because the varieties most commonly sold in the UK have been bred to survive travel. Inside, they have tough, pulpy pockets that hold the seeds of the fruit and these don't break down so easily in cooking.

Unless they are the freshest, most flavoursome varieties, tomatoes should be skinned by soaking them in boiling water and have the pockets and seeds removed. Otherwise a useful trick used in much Catalan cooking, is to slice them horizontally, scoop out the pips and pockets and grate the flesh into your dish.

If you are going to serve them with a breakfast or mixed grill, turn them upside down and squeeze them flat in the pan so that the whole lot gets well fried. The oozing tomatoey sweetness soaks up all the oils and goey flavours from the meats. If they are the freshest of the fresh from Italy or your neighbour's greenhouse, with that powerful grassy smell from the stalk, then of course you should just eat them whole with a little sea salt.

Artichokes

There are two varieties of artichoke, which couldn't be more different; in fact, there is no connection between them at all. The Jerusalem artichoke's original name was *girasole*, the Italian word for sunflower. They are knobbly little root vegetables which, when peeled and boiled, are great as soup or made into a seasoned purée. They are much mistrusted because of their tendency to cause flatulence – which they do, but are nonetheless unjustly neglected. When mashed, their nutty flavour gives the most comforting, buttery

complement to strong, red meat. It you want to skin them, it's easiest to do so after they are cooked, when the papery skin rubs off to the touch. When raw and sliced paper thin, they perk up a salad no end.

Globe artichokes when picked small (no more than six centimetres across) can be sliced in half, pan-fried in butter with lots of salt and eaten with your fingers. As they get older, you need to boil or steam them until the centre or heart is soft. Then you just pick the outer leaves off one by one, dip them in melted butter or a vinaigrette and suck the flesh off the end. Eventually you will reach the tender heart, which can be eaten greedily.

Peppers

The capsicum family, as they are properly known, are members of the same family as Deadly Nightshade and are used for their many different properties across the world. The most common peppers we see in our shops are the yellow, green and red bell peppers and the red sweet peperoncini. They are milder in nature than many of their hot sisters, such as the jalapeño, banana, chilli and habañero peppers. You need to experiment with what you find available and what your palate can handle.

Like tomatoes, unless you are buying these fresh from the market or in hot Mediterranean countries, they are typically rather watery and tasteless. Cooking them simply releases more water into your dish, while their thick skins are difficult to break down. To draw out the best flavour from peppers, burn the skin black all over until it blisters, either over a naked flame or under the grill. Pop them in the fridge or freezer to cool, then the skin will peel off easily. You can slice them straight into a salad, have them on their own or add them to a dish such as ratatouille. The difference in preparing them this way is considerable and worth the trouble.

Aubergines

It was always thought you should slice aubergines, or egg plants, and sprinkle them with salt before weighing them down in a colander. The same is true with cucumber. The reasons are twofold. Firstly, older varieties could be slightly bitter, and this drained out the bitter juices; with modern varieties, this is unnecessary. Secondly it was to get the water out. Though this isn't entirely necessary, it rather depends on what you want to do with them as it does prevent them becoming waterlogged during cooking. Aubergines are also hugely absorbent, taking in almost their own weight in oil as they start to break down during cooking. To avoid this, slice or cube them into a bowl, sprinkle over some salt and oil, then turn them over with your hands to make sure they all have a light covering. Then you can just put them in the oven, lightly fry or poach them in a little stock, lemon juice and garlic. Unless you are cooking the aubergine whole, for say a salad or simply fried, peel off some of the skin as it reduces the bitterness.

Mushrooms

A whole chapter could be written about edible fungi and there are many books that will guide you through the more exotic and gastronomic varieties.

The mushrooms you are most likely to encounter as you start your foodie journey are the ubiquitous chestnut or closed-cup mushrooms. Mostly the farmed mushrooms we find available are grown on straw and are pretty clean. It is wholly unnecessary to skin them, just get rid of any excess peat. These mushrooms can almost always be cooked any old how but it does make a big difference to their flavour if you slice them and fry them in a big sauté pan so that they don't touch each other. This seals them and prevents them from drying out.

The big field or Portobello mushrooms can be grilled or baked but have lots of moisture.

Mushrooms like ceps, morel, *girolles* and *porcini*, which you will find in specialist shops, are abounding in wild and intense flavours which they can impart to any dish. If you buy them dried, don't forget to soak them first and then rinse them to get rid of the grit. You can cook them whole in something saucy or slice them into oil, season with pepper and garlic and let them reduce a bit.

Courgettes, Marrows and Cucumbers

When these are cooked for too long, they can become slushy and tasteless. There are ways to counter this. For courgettes, add a sprinkling of stock powder and cook them with a little water but so that they still have a bite.

Marrows are basically overgrown courgettes and can also be a bit flavourless. Scooping out the seeds and stuffing the marrow with a rich rice and tomato mixture and then slicing it makes an impressive vegetarian dish. Otherwise, skin and slice them, then sautée in butter with lots of salt and pepper until they are golden. This keeps them firm and delicious.

Cucumbers have long been making traditional appearances in salad or sandwiches as sliced rounds. Try something different. You can sprinkle them with salt and press the liquid out of them, as with aubergines. Then peeled and sliced longways, they're a bit more interesting lightly stir-fried.

Pumpkin and Squashes

There are endless varieties of squash, the most common being butternut, which has a rich, eggy taste. The Delicata squash has a texture much like sweet potato. Mostly you can just peel these, remove the pips (which can be roasted separately with salt), slice them up in wedges or rounds and roast them. They can also be mashed and puréed and are perfect ballast for a creamy soup. The smaller squashes can be cooked whole without peeling, then just cut open at the table and eaten with butter and black pepper.

Pumpkins are pretty tough when they are big, so stick to the small ones – except for making lanterns. Their natural oil exudes a vanilla and malt aroma when baked, and the seeds can also be cleaned and roasted with salt, then sprinkled on soup or salads. Pumpkin pie is, of course, a Thanksgiving favourite, and in North Africa they mash pumpkin with rose flower water and cinnamon.

Endive

Sometimes called chicory, Belgian chicory or witloof, endive is a tulip-shaped bulb made up of tightly packed leaves. It can be served as salad or sliced in half longways and baked or sautéed gently with butter. Red chicory has a smoky flavour when cooked in the same way, or it can be finely shredded as a salad leaf. This is not to be confused with curly endive, another kind of bitter salad leaf from the same family.

Fennel

This is a versatile and aromatic vegetable, as good served raw with oil, salt and fresh bread as it is braised, or sliced and wedged under a chicken when roasting. Finely sliced, you can pop it into the cavity of a whole baked fish, when it lends a fine aniseed aroma. Slightly burned in butter and then blended with lemon juice, fennel brings magic to any soup combination. This is a vegetable that responds well to surprising companions, such as sausages and mackerel.

Preparing Seafood

When you gaze into the window of the fish shop, you may experience a mixture of confusion, revulsion, excitement or terror. The sloopy tentacles of an octopus or grinning teeth of a conger eel might well be enough to put you off for ever. But steel yourself. Fish is almost the easiest thing to prepare and cook; you just have to be careful with the bones. Fish are also amazingly accommodating for the new cook.

When it comes to supermarkets, you should avoid buying their fish unless they have a stated sustainable fish policy. Being labelled equivocally as being 'line-caught' or 'within sustainable quotas' doesn't always mean anything. All fish would be sustainable if we let them be for a while. But it's all to do with where and how they are caught. We've overdone fishing in most of the world. Now, the pioneering Marine Stewardship Council (MSC) has established a set of criteria by which sustainable fishing can be measured. Look out for their brand.

Clearly there are also fears around the intensive over-farming of fish, characterised by the examples of deformed salmon, fed on fish meal and weaned on hormones. But this situation has changed over the last decade since the early abuses, and seriously responsible farming of many species of fish has taken over.

But it isn't all gloomy; this situation has given rise to the appearance of many minor stars of the sea which you can eat without feeling too guilty. Mackerel, sardines and herring are all magically oily fish and so naturally very good for you. And some previously unknown bystanders are taking the main stage. Pollock, coley, whiting, gunard and megrim, with the right coaxing, are as good as any other fish. Sure, they are not all as obviously desirable as the big stars of the sea, but isn't it better to wait for a bit to be sure we have wild Dover sole, halibut, whitebait and plaice again? My advice is to find yourself a fishmonger you like and trust and who will help you start to buy sustainable seafood that will test your abilities.

Fish are slimy by nature. They actually secrete a protein from their bodies to keep themselves clean, but a scaling and wash under cold running water will fix that. Personally, I can't really see any advantage to cleaning your own fish unless you happen to have caught it yourself. So let your fishmonger do the dirty work and scale and gut it for you.

Providing they're dead, fish will allow you to do almost anything to them, and because their flesh is so simple, they generally require very little cooking. And they look good at the table. The fresher they are, the more this is the case. Nothing gives the feeling of freshness more than scooping the steaming, herb-infused flesh from a whole fish.

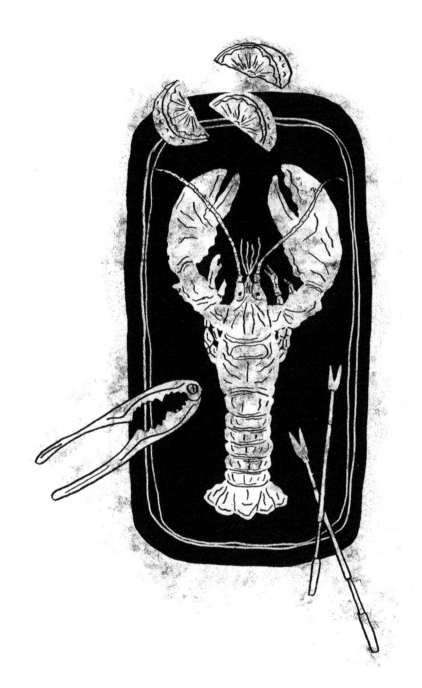

Alternatively, the fishmonger will ask you whether you want the fish to be filleted from the bone or, if you are buying meat from a big fish such as tuna or swordfish, it will usually be cut into steaks. Both of these make rationing simple when you are cooking for large numbers or don't know how hungry people will be.

Once you get it home, you should store fish flat on a low shelf in the coldest part of the fridge while you decide how to cook it. Don't let whole fish sit around in its packaging for too long. Lay it on a plate and let it get air around it.

Ideally, you should cook and eat fish on the day you buy it, but if you can't, fish is something that freezes pretty well, and it defrosts quite quickly so that you can bring it out as and when you need it. But bear in mind that most fish has been frozen at sea before hitting the fish markets, so quality and freshness are always an issue. You'll soon learn to tell the difference between a long-haul catch and a fish straight from the sea. The skin is firmer and the eyes brighter.

In terms of cooking, pan-fried, grilled or baked fish are the standards. And because, unlike meat, the flesh is not complex, having few inner workings such as sinews and tendons, it is simple to cook and it really picks up the flavours and aromas of what you add to it. The best way to decide what you are going to do to a bit of fish is to gather your ingredients round you and think about how they will best complement each other.

In addition to the old favourites and the newcomers we've mentioned, salmon and trout remain hugely popular. Salmon are anadromous, which means they spawn in fresh water and migrate into the sea. Wild salmon in Britain are a rare treat worth every penny – if you can find them. But North Atlantic salmon fished off Iceland have much denser, redder meat. Sea trout is usually available in late spring, caught as they come upstream into British rivers. Brown and rainbow trout are freshwater fish and much more delicate in flesh and flavour. Again, shop responsibly.

More recently, with the changing tastes that come with new cultures, other freshwater fish such as carp and perch have been more readily available. They are often bony but with really smooth, buttery flesh. Pike, thankfully seldom found and also rather bony, has a muddy taste. You can cook it in a cheese sauce.

As long as you follow a few simple rules, shellfish isn't difficult to prepare and cook either, although picking up some expert knowledge does help. You can learn from your fishmonger or a knowledgeable writer on seafood; Rick Stein is my favourite and he lives close to the seafood he works with.

The hysteria about food poisoning is somewhat overstated. The potential danger arises because you have to cook shellfish fresh so that they are still alive, or they putrefy in their shells, and that's when they become toxic and cause illness. But they also concentrate toxins from sea-water and are purified before being sold so should never be eaten straight from the sea.

Small shellfish will stay alive as long as the valve on their shells remains intact. Sometimes, if they have been wrenched too harshly from their marine lodgings, the shell gets damaged or the valve is rendered useless, which is why you occasionally find them open when you get them home. So, before cooking check them over and bin the dodgy ones. You can keep them fairly fresh in the fridge or briefly in the freezer. Otherwise make sure they are clean then apply heat – steam, boiling water, a hot grill – and they will open, aromatic, fishy and fresh, ready to pop in your mouth.

Crustaceans are even easier to cook but the larger they are and the more limbs they have, the more tricky it is to extract the meat. In the main, unless you feel very brave, you might forgo cooking crabs and lobsters at home to begin with. Leave that to the professional kitchens with lots of ventilation and large pots of boiling water ready to accommodate their victims. An essential aspect to cooking is to leave some treats worth going out for, after all. But prawns, langoustines, crayfish and their other leggy chums are quick and easy to cook. They conveniently quickly go pink when they are ready – boiled, grilled, baked, whatever. And with them, there is little you need do and the simpler your ambition, the more likely you are to succeed.

Preparing Meat

Meat is as it looks: blood and guts. Some men might revert to hunter-gatherer when they look into a butcher's window, ripping their shirts open and beating their chests with clenched fists. Others may wince mildly at the more visceral exhibits on sale.

Either way, you need to know that you are actually eating dead animals, which have been killed for the benefit of our appetites, and that pretty much all parts of them are nourishing and wholesome, from brains to trotters – 'everything but the squeak'. That is except the fatty bits, which are very highly saturated and potentially problematic for people with cholesterol or heart issues. The one unifying thing with meat is that, with the exception of pork rind which we turn into crackling, we don't eat the skin. Instead we turn it into leather and wear it or enrol it into some other more exotic activities.

Anyone who wants to know about meat, how it is produced and what to do with it should read Hugh Fearnley-Whittingstall's *Meat*. He is more than expert, he is a flesh hero and writes with a passion and love for his subject.

If you have bought meat from the supermarket, again get it out of the packaging as quickly as possible and drain away any blood or water. Though it's dead, meat likes to breathe cleanly. Dry it off, cover it or rub it with cooking oil and put it back in the fridge until you want to cook it.

The first thing to understand about meat is that, unlike fish, it has a vastly complex structure, with nerves, muscles, cartilage, sinews and tendons. These require breaking down by cooking. The more there are, the longer it will take for the cut to break down and release its flavours. But don't be fooled. Just because a piece of meat may look clean and simple – the most obvious being a piece of fillet steak – doesn't determine the depth of potential flavour.

There are some fairly simple rules of thumb which will help you along the way. The less fine cuts of meat, which have a lot of muscle to break down and come from places such as the shoulder (or chuck) or leg where a lot of stewing or braising meat comes from, will need slow cooking to make the meat tender. The least attractive bits of an animal, such as say the tail of a cow, which is all fat, tail vertebrae and gristle, when cooked long enough yields the most potent flavours and tasty meat picked from its bones. There is nothing more reviving than a bowl of oxtail soup.

The next thing is how to choose what you want to eat. Meat can be fatty, lean, gristly, on the bone, filleted, rolled, chopped, racked, minced, made into sausages, smoked, air-dried, cured and so on. But getting to know the cuts of meat and how to handle them takes practice. To a large extent you need to be led by your curiosity and experience, using your judgement and the aid of your butcher to learn what's from where on a beast and how it will cook. If you are in a restaurant and try something new that you haven't cooked at home, just ask about it. The aspiring cook should never be frightened to ask questions, and you'll find that professionals like butchers and chefs love to be given a chance to show off their expertise. Who doesn't?

The finest cuts of meat, that is those that have least fat or other tissues, are taken from the rump or loin of the animal. Because they are leaner and the meat is more tender, they require much less cooking. The tenderloin is where the finest cuts come, then the rib. These are known as steaks from beef and chops from lamb and pork. You will have your favourite cut of steak, from the T-bone to *chateaubriand*, and their differences do lend well to the ways you plan to cook them. A sirloin, which has more fat, responds better to being well cooked, whereas a lean fillet will just dry out. But in the end you should pay no attention to what others think. Just cook meat – like anything else – exactly as you like it, from blue to frazzled. No shame. Just pleasure.

Apart from a rare steak, fat is crucial in cooking meat, whether it's mince and sausages or a large joint or rib. It's essential for retaining juiciness and flavour and for breaking down the tougher elements of the cut. The best butchers should give you a piece of meat with just the right amount of fat to cook it properly. Lean cuts may help build muscle or reduce cholesterol, but to enrich flavours in cooking you need to let the fat help the cooking process. So leave it on and drain it away after cooking (even better, you can keep it for cooking later).

You will notice in some restaurants that the flesh in the centre of a rare or blue steak is sometimes cold. This is not right and is because it has been taken straight from the fridge to the pan. For obvious reasons, meat doesn't conduct heat well. If it did, we'd all cook in hot weather. So for cuts that need fast cooking, meat should be at room temperature, rather than cold, when you start to cook. This reduces the cooking time and means that the meat will have reached the right temperature throughout.

When you are preparing pork joints, because they have such thick skin, you need to heave them from the fridge before you go to bed or when you go to work, so you can leave them to dry out. Rubbing pork skin with salt will afford you a wickedly crispy and sticky crackling and the meat will cook evenly. Pork chops and bigger cuts, like a beef rib or leg of lamb, will also benefit from a few hours out of the fridge and vigorous rubbing with your own favourite seasonings.

Cheap cuts from low-price supermarkets sourced at factory farms are to be discouraged. It is surely better to go vegetarian than waste money on the flesh of an animal that hasn't lived a decent life. After slaughter, they are very often pumped with water to make them look lean and plump in their cheap wrapping. You will notice that the meat exudes lots of liquid and reduces in size radically with cooking.

Try baking a pre-packed gammon joint and see just how it shrinks.

Because of the complex molecular structure of meat, stewing can often have the opposite effect than you expect, as being cooked in water can make meat tougher by flushing out its natural juices and fats. However, during the long, slow cooking required for casseroles, stews and pot-roasts a liquidy exchange takes place and the flavours and moisture of the meat, stock and vegetables merge. To bring added flavour to the early stages of a dish like this, many cooks often coat meat in flour and brown the outside, causing a caramelising effect. This process adds richer flavours to the dish by starting a chemical reaction between the amino acids and sugar in the meat. It does not, however, as it is commonly thought, 'seal' the flavours in the meat.

For stews and casseroles, it is always best to buy a whole piece of meat and cut it up yourself, getting rid of any too gristly bits. Even if it is a bit more expensive, you can see what you are getting. Again, don't cut away the fat entirely. Beef skirt steak or shoulder, or lamb chuck is perfect for this.

Preparing joints for roasting, unless it's best well-hung pedigree beef or new-season lamb, requires some thought about how you want to retain or even introduce juiciness and flavour. Here you can be as creative as you like in preparing some kind of herby, spicy, buttery, fruity, garlicky, boozy concoction to pour over the meat, slip under the skin or insert into incisions in the flesh.

Marinating is another way to prepare meat for fast cooking, say on a barbecue or if you want to end up with something very tender. Marinades often include lemon juice, which partly cooks the meat and the other ingredients, while infusing it with a powerful richness, as with Japanese teriyaki, for example. The Italians have a dish called *brasato*, which is a long cut of beef or veal soaked in vinegar or red wine for a couple of days before cooking. There are many other versions the world over.

You should always remember that pre-packed meats, such as are found ready sliced or vacuum-sealed, have been processed in some way. Of course, you can have no control over what goes into sausages, the provenance of bacon or how it is cured, but it is always worth looking at the labels to check what other ingredients are contained in your meat products. Vote with your feet. Walk to the butcher and ask questions about what and where your food comes from and how it died. Never accept second best.

When it comes to offal, you need to start with the obvious: liver and kidneys. The visceral quality of innards means that they can smell pretty vile when you cook them. So if you don't have a kitchen with a door or windows to the outside world and you start making your own haggis or boiling a sheep's head, you'll be living in a house addled with the overpowering smell of animal. Think glue factory.

Notwithstanding the traditionally low status of kidneys and liver on the menu, they should be prepared as if they will be served fit for a royal banquet. The most readily available are livers from calves, lambs and pigs, and kidneys from lambs. The smaller the animal they are from, the tastier they are likely to be. Once you get home, keep your bits well chilled until you are ready to cook them. If your butcher hasn't already, cut away any unnecessary or unattractive bits. Liver responds well to being sliced thinly and soaked in milk for a while before cooking. With kidneys you need to leave a little of the fat – or suet – around them, as it helps to keep them moist during cooking.

The main advice here is to find a reliable butcher near you, soon. Don't necessarily be fooled by a lavish window display. Follow your nose. If it smells fresh and looks clean and welcoming, that is more important. Observe if there are off-cuts lying around. Next pay attention to how much pre-packed produce they stock; the best butchers won't. Ask them about the provenance of the beasts they buy and whether the meat is hung. Well-hung meat is more tender because the lactic acid present at the time of death continues to work on breaking down muscle tissue. So you might be looking for something that has aged almost a month since slaughter. The finest beef is dry-aged in special units but it's hard to get hold of and is very expensive.

Before we move on, we should just think for a moment about the responsibility of being meat-eaters. You need to be clear in your mind that what you are eating was a happy, satisfied, well looked after beast and that it was humanely killed for you to eat. Don't underestimate how much farmers and butchers love their animals. You need to love your livestock if you are going to kill it properly. Many butchers will write the name of the farm on the wall and some know the name of the animal. Even a busy butcher will be pleased to answer questions about the provenance of their stock and prepare any specialist cuts of meats you want. If they aren't or won't, find another who is. And if you ask nicely, a really helpful butcher might even sharpen your knives for you (but be aware, it is a criminal offence in some places to carry knives).

One last word about veal. If it wasn't consumed, most new-born calves would be destroyed at birth. However, in Britain, always at the forefront of animal welfare, we became quite rightly very squeamish about eating veal. And it is a controversial subject. The rearing and production process goes against the grain. Keeping calves in crates in darkness and feeding them on powdered milk is horrific. However, an increasing number of calves are being reared for rosé veal. This means that they live in daylight in open barns; some are even weaned outside on 'nursing' cows, which means their lives are even happier. Do ask your butcher for rosé veal. As a meat-eater, it is a responsible thing to do. You will encourage better animal husbandry and more rosé veal will become available on the market.

Preparing Poultry and Game

Birds are a different kettle of fish. As instruments of flight, they can be particularly sinewy. They require careful cooking. However, most of the birds we eat today couldn't fly even if they wanted to. If they are lucky enough to have access to the sky, we tend to feed them sufficiently well to keep them weighted down on *terra firma*. We have even trained some of them to waddle up to the farmer's wife in a sophisticated act of avian suicide, so that she can over-feed their livers, which she later removes to be served to the delectation of overpaid humans as *foie gras.*

It is important to foreground the main arguments about poultry at the beginning of this section because too many people are still ignoring the facts as they stand. After the Second World War and the nightmares of rationing, which lasted well into the 1950s, food production had intensified and new ways of feeding a hungry nation were being developed. Hence the curse of farming – mass production and industrialisation.

Gone were the milking stools and churns from which the milk was sold locally and turned into butter. And turkeys, like insane, ugly Parisian widows, were raised from incubator to doom in sinister, dark sheds; thousands of them living in vile stink and deafening jibberish. A worse indignity to be visited on any living thing is hard to imagine.

The moral turpitude of mass turkey farming in the 1960s was nothing compared to the tortures cooked up for their smaller cousin. What a disgusting record of human advancement this has been. Countless diseased, deranged and deformed fowl, locked up in cages, unable to move any body part but their necks to peck at food made from their own ground-down carcasses. Stuffed full of antibiotics and growth hormones, these birds live a matter of weeks and are genetically modified to get from egg to table in record time. These miserable birds have had nothing resembling a life, so can give nothing back in terms of taste. No matter how poor you are, you get what you pay for. A diseased, miserable fowl will cost nothing and give nothing. Chicken was a luxury product until battery farming. Let it be so again, so that we have to learn to get the best out of it.

Having said that, even free-range farmers seldom let chickens live long enough in the UK. To be really flavoursome, chickens need to have been allowed to live sufficiently long for their fat to begin to age. Traditionally these might be old boiling fowl used for *coq au vin*, where the birds are leaner and the meat is stronger. As with most things culinary, the French have got it right. Though they are no strangers to battery farming, some of the tastiest chickens in the world come from France.

The *poulet de Bresse* has been protected in France since the 1950s and farms are limited in the numbers they can rear. It is a benchmark of quality. *Poulet noir* are also worth searching out. And here in Britain, there are also some properly run chicken farms, selling mature birds full of rich flavour and dense flesh, for example Cornish Red or Light Sussex.

The rule of thumb is that you should be paying two or three times more for a chicken than you think you should. Then you'll be getting something approaching decent, with bags of flavour and enough life in its bones to make a really good stock.

As we have started to master once again the husbandry of chickens, so high-quality farmed duck and geese have become increasingly available. The same rules apply as with chicken and turkey. Find something well bred, looked after in life and worthy in death. Once again, you need to consult with your butcher. They should know where the bird comes from and, most importantly, will sell it with the giblets which, as we'll discover later, are essential.

You will also find farmed quail around. They are now fed on midges, the curse of the Scottish Highlands, so I think we should encourage their breeding. They don't require much doing to them at all, and like poussin (spring chickens) are best spatchcocked – sliced down the middle – and cooked flat on a griddle, though you can also stuff them with something interesting, if so inclined.

Game birds, the most common of which are wood pigeon, pheasant, wild duck, partridge and grouse, are all small and bony. And because they have actually been able to use their wings to fly, unlike their domestic cousins, they can be chewier.

A fail-safe way to prepare game birds for cooking is to joint them, keeping only the really tasty bits (the legs and breast), although this can get a bit finicky.

If you do find yourself buying a wild goose, you should be asking some questions. They are mostly protected worldwide and, if not, should only be shot in season, on the wing. They are a culinary challenge and have a very fishy, strong flavour, drying out easily during cooking.

Though you don't need to go to extremes, most game birds do benefit from hanging around for a bit as it softens the flesh. But sadly, most are no longer actually 'hung' as they used to be, so it's best to leave them to breathe in the back of the fridge for a week, where they acquire a nicely intensified gaminess.

In terms of preparation, there is no set piece for poultry and game birds. You need to look at the bird (if you find yourself looking it in the eye, then chop its head off) to assess its body weight and how much fat there is. Ducks and geese tend to be quite lardy, so you will need to make sure that the fat is able to escape. Game birds might need the addition of some bacon or fat to keep them moist.

There are many different ways to ensure crispy skin, from the famous scene of the early celebrity chef Fanny Craddock on television pinching the skin of a duck with her long, painted, bejewelled fingers, to pricking turkey with a fork, placing bacon over the breast or pasting a herby mixture under the skin. Frankly, this is where trial and error will be your best friends. But a fail-safe is to get your bird out of the fridge long enough to bring it up to room temperature, then rub the skin with salt and let it dry a little. You can make incisions all over the bird and pop anything in the holes, such as garlic, lemon, herbs, soy sauce, honey, wine – anything to bring in flavour. The bigger the bird is, the more help it will need. A little chicken or game bird doesn't really need much except to ensure that it doesn't dry out.

This is just some of the thinking you need to do when deciding how to buy and prepare a bird for cooking. If you care where they are from, take care of them before cooking and find the right accompaniments, you'll find cooking them a quick route to success in the kitchen.

Success in Your Kitchen

If you have got this far, then the really exciting bit is about to start. And if, until now, you have thought of cooking as an enigma, the mist is going to clear. You have the perfect cooking vessels at hand, the right implements to marshal them into action and the ingredients are prepared and ready to be cast into the cauldron. Now you start to turn them into something you are going to enjoy eating. The alchemy begins.

First you have to decide how you are going to cook the ingredients you have. Or are you going to cook them at all? Is it the right moment to compose one of your fine salads accompanied by a delicate dressing? Do you need something in a pot to last you all week? Are you entertaining a friend or a lover? Have you got something on the turn which needs to be used up? If you need inspiration, might it be an opportunity to check what your favourite food writer has to say? Now's the time to ask the questions for which you're going to give a resounding response.

The simplest thing of all to understand about cooking is that most kinds of dish are made in the same way but just with different ingredients. This section of the book takes you on a stroll across the most popular ways of cooking simple dishes, from soups and roasts to pâtés to puddings, to give you an insight into both the techniques and the possibilities as they present themselves.

These are not dishes presented as you may be used to finding them, but this way you will learn far more about what to do with food and how to cook it. Cooking, particularly when it involves baking or more complex styles, can be a precise art. But once you have the confidence to cook what you like, then you can start using the really exciting recipes in your favourite books. By that stage you'll also want to make your own additions and amendments.

Here you will understand how to combine the ingredients you have prepared and to cook dishes intuitively in ways that work for you. Like all things in life, you will learn by your successes and your mistakes.

A Word About Heat

For lots of people, the regulator knobs or dials on their ovens and hobs have two settings: on and off. You quickly need to understand how subtle the impact of flames or magnetically induced heat can be (I am assuming that most aspiring chefs will have thrown off the shackles of the electric ring which is, in fact, either on or off). Gradual increases or reductions of heat can make the difference between something working or not. And if you are preparing a meal for others, when you want everything to appear perfectly cooked at the same time, you need to understand the ways heat works.

The best cooking machines for learning this lesson were the traditional ranges, fired from one source and never regulated. Cookers like the Aga are the most common version of this, and on them you can learn about heating ingredients at different levels, starting them off, moving them around and finishing them without ever turning a dial. But most of us don't have access to these and we're using either gas or electricity. So it is worth reading the guide to your oven and hob, to understand the settings of your oven and cooker: just where is the heat coming from; how it is circulating around or conducting through your food; which hob will be best for simmering slowly; how fast does the grill element change heat? And so on.

You also need a grasp on the differences between the ways you can apply heat. Knowing when it's better to steam, poach, boil, fry, bake, roast or grill are key instincts you will acquire over time. Each has their virtues and dangers and again you need to take risks. But don't despair, the people who can precisely boil an egg or produce uniformly roast potatoes won't be the same as those who can whip up a dazzling stir-fry or delectable soup. You find the things that work for you. Let the ingredients guide you. You will look at a floret of broccoli and it will just come to you to pan-fry it, briefly boil it or even pop it in the microwave.

There are broadly three approaches to cooking with heat: in the oven, using water, or frying. You can combine these at different stages of preparing a dish but it's worth knowing what happens in terms of heat.

When you cook something in the oven, it is surrounded by heat, so is usually, except for grilling, being cooked from all sides (though many ovens have a wide range of settings, this is really always the case, except the intensity changes). This is perfect for dishes that need to be cooked gently, like vegetables or casseroles; carefully, like meringues or soufflés; hot and consistently, like bread or pies; or those that have various stages, like a roast.

Using water for poaching, boiling or steaming helps to keep the flavours and nutritional value in any food. We've moved on from the days of just boiling every vegetable, so steaming is more common as a way of cooking vegetables and fish. I don't recommend steaming chicken, as it actually has the reverse effect of drying out the moisture in the flesh. And most light, green vegetables can be nicely done in the microwave, with a few centimetres of water. Poaching has gone out of fashion as a means of cooking but is a nice way to prepare fish, with the addition of a little wine and some herbs.

As you experiment in the kitchen, you will mainly be cooking on the hob in your big sauté pan. This is when you have most control, not so much at the mercy of forgetful mistakes. Dishes can turn out exactly as you want. Braising, sautéing, pan-frying and stir-frying offer the quickest and best results and crucially allow you to see the ingredients as they metamorphose, allowing you the greatest opportunity to make subtle alterations or even drastic changes. Once you get used to cooking with different oils and butter and regulating the heat, the next thing that will come naturally is the ability to understand instinctively what to add and when to leave well alone.

What Goes Together

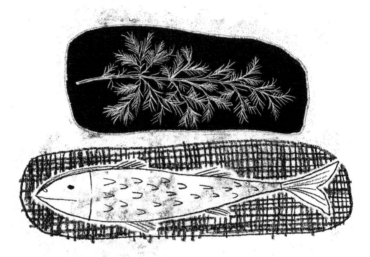

There are really no secrets to being a great cook, other than trial and error, imagination, willingness to experiment and quick wits when it all goes wrong. Enthusiasm will take you a long way before you need to start worrying about the exact temperature at which to cook *foie gras* or rise the perfect soufflé. Even then you can make a studied guess and find success comes surprisingly quickly through trial and error.

Having said that, there are some tricks of the trade to the creating of any dish that usually go unmentioned if you are slavishly following a recipe. These may seem rather obvious but are essential bits of knowledge that will transform your ability to develop a highly individual and inspired approach to cooking.

Knowing what goes together is down to personal taste and experience, of course, but there is also a compendium of flavours, colours and textures that it does you well to understand. There are obvious contenders such as lamb and mint, pea and ham, fish and dill, but the scope goes far beyond that, so that you could be pairing mackerel with rhubarb and onion with oranges. You'll find a clever manual of these combinations in Niki Segnit's *The Flavour Thesaurus* (Bloomsbury). Here she goes into detail about how different flavours match each other. It's the perfect book for cooking without recipes because it's like having a reference book to check your own ideas against, or to give you a splash of inspiration.

If you just want to try things out on your own, you need to think about what your ingredients taste like before they are cooked, how that will change and what effect they might have on the produce they are being cooked with. When you are standing at your preparation area or staring into the fridge or cupboards in the kitchen, you need to think of how things complement and flatter each other. When can something quite dull be titivated by a thrilling accompaniment? How might you cook something slightly differently in order to avoid the usual outcome? Knowing how human taste works does help. Basically we don't like too much of the same texture, colour or flavour. Which is why so much oriental food is so exciting to us. Because each individual element has been prepared and designed to accompany and bring out the best in the others.

Ultimately you need to be able to think like this, but to start with there are a number of things just to avoid. For instance, the human palate cannot endure too much oil or fat. You need to provide some sharp, acidic accompaniment to an oily fish that will cut through it, or put a strong aromatic vegetable with fatty lamb or mutton. It's why we often cook a bird such as duck with citrus fruits.

Equally, no-one likes to eat things that are too uniform in texture or colour. Dishes that are too saucy, creamy or silky to the taste need something to offset them. We like to bite into something substantial as well as having the sensation of delicate tastes melting in our mouths. So scattering toasted nuts into a bowl of Brussels sprouts, or adding some finely chopped mint and croûtons to your painfully pale celeriac soup, are transformational gestures that will never go unnoticed. An enthusiasm for roasting vegetables has developed in recent years and is a brilliant, easy success for a cook. You toss them all into a roasting pan, coated in oil and seasonings, and leave them to glaze, crisp and caramelise. When you fish them out of the oven, they look bold and interesting. But beware; parsnip, carrot, swede and beetroot all have the same texture when cooked like this. Just like your roast potatoes. So to bring your meal alive you might want to mix something green and freshly steamed into them. Or surprise your guests by chopping them up roughly and serving them with chicory leaves and dressing as a salad.

Don't be frightened to try outlandish combinations or turn dishes inside out like this. We are often hidebound by our traditions more than we need to be. By the time you are confident enough to be playing about with ingredients in the ways that give you pleasure, it simply doesn't matter how a dish turns up at the table. After all, it's exactly what the famous food experimenters do. They shock and surprise the expectations of our palates. Do the same.

What follows is not a comprehensive list of things you can cook but a series of examples of dishes that represent the style, ingredients and attitude to cooking, encouraged in this book. Make what you will of what is included. But mostly what you want is to strike out and give yourself a chance. Follow your senses.

Cooking for Friends

Entertaining has that air of duty about it and the whole notion of it rings fear for many people because they forget one simple concept. First and foremost, it's about seeing your inner circle and sharing your table with them. Being invited for a meal ought to be about enjoying good food without fuss. The important bit is convivial, inclusive conversation and the gentle imbibing of a top drop of wine. Too often, dinner parties are ruined by hosts taxing themselves in the kitchen to the point that you never see them, and the whole evening becomes drearily dominated by the whole cooking performance. Which is attention-seeking and boring, even for enthusiasts.

While it's important for cooks to test themselves and their abilities, unless it's actually advertised as a fine dining experience, then all you need to create is a well-balanced meal with sufficiently interesting flavours and quantities that your guests will feel replete and impressed that you have fed them so well.

Timing is essential in cooking, so if you eat in your kitchen, then it's perfectly possible to be entertaining and to cook at the same time. But even so, you don't want to be clattering and scraping while everyone is talking; poise and control are always impressive qualities of deportment. If it looks as though you're serving beguiling dishes with effortless ease, everyone will be satisfied. If the atmosphere is stressful, you will cause discomfort. The atmosphere is stressful when the cook is obviously trying too hard or the whole meal is depending on a high-stakes outcome.

A starter of raw fennel, lumps of Parmesan and salami will be much easier to control, while you're getting the main dishes ready. Preparing a cold soup, served from the table with some hot, toasted croûtons, will distract the company enough to get them eating while you're concentrating on other things.

When it comes to the centrepiece of your meal, don't always go for the obvious. Think about how your favourite restaurants and cafés abroad serve the food you like. Have the vegetables as a separate course or deliver them to the table like a salad with vinaigrette dressing. Keep the table interesting and involve people in it, perhaps with a shared pot to dip into or combinations to explore. And be aware of who is at the table. Don't give your ageing great uncle a tiny quail to eat from the bone; or if you are giving each guest a whole fish, make sure their plates are not cluttered with other things.

Finally a word to the wise about wine. Of course people should bring wine when you are inviting them to a meal, but if you've gone to a lot of trouble with your cooking, you'll want to be in charge of which wine balances with those flavours. So supply your own. Unless they've asked what you want them to bring to drink, politely thank your guests and tell them you'll look forward to enjoying it another time. Chances are if folk have brought an excellent bottle, they'll expect you to keep it anyway. And there is nothing that gives you a worse hangover than the competing impurities of different grape varieties.

A Pot of Soup

On a chilly winter's day or a balmy summer evening, soup is king. Versatile, endless in variety, soup is a matchless potion. Whether a thin, reviving broth for recuperation or a hearty mess of potage, it can be sustaining and refreshing, welding to any occasion with untroubled ease.

By rights, soup should come last in the list of dishes you learn to cook because it is so often made from what went before. But when it comes to cooking, there is nothing simpler and more satisfying to make and you will see instant results. So it needs to be at the beginning of the learning curve to encourage your enthusiasms to grow. Like all cooking, give yourself free rein to be creative. You can always taste the love in a pot of soup.

Soup needs three things: a large pan, ingredients and stock. There is no point making a small quantity of soup; it can last for days or be licked clean from the plate before you have time to share any with a friend or freeze it for a rainy Saturday. Soup can be made from almost anything you like and is a perfect way to use up leftovers or unwanted ingredients about to pass their best.

You don't even have to know what kind of soup you are creating until it is done. The only thing you probably need to decide early on is the consistency you are aiming for. Is it going to be a hearty soup with chunky vegetables and grains or pulses, or a smooth creamy soup, puréed with your hand blender or liquidiser? The addition of pulses like beans, or a grain such as barley, can happen on a whim. And, because there are no rules, sometimes soup can be all of these.

Stock

Stock is a fail-safe kitchen preparation for the newcomer to cooking. It's a culinary chrysalis from which a beautiful butterfly can emerge. Making stock can make you feel like an expert in a matter of hours. The mix of water, vegetables and fish, poultry or meat you use will create anything from a delicate bouillon to a dark consommé. Like all cooking, stock can become a bit of an art form because it is used as the basis for so many different dishes. But for the newcomer about the kitchen, you need to head for a winner. Don't get too complicated. It's more important that you become instinctive about saving bones and carcasses to use them for making stock than overcomplicating the matter.

So given that the most likely circumstance is a leftover bird, usually a chicken, into your big pan it goes. Throw everything remaining from the bird (including any raw bits or giblets) into the pan, including all the bits that have been chewed, sucked and scraped from every plate. Cover the whole with water, add carrot, celery, onion or leek – all chopped – sea salt, a few black peppercorns and bay leaves. Bring to the boil and simmer for as long as you like. Cook it fast if you prefer a light chicken broth for which it's worth being ill in bed.

When you think that it has a flavour all of its own, strain it into a vessel and pop in the fridge. When cold, the stock will become jellified from the bones, and the fat will condense and harden at the surface overnight. This can be left until you use the stock (which can last for more than a week) or removed before freezing.

The same can be done with meat bones and, once you've got the hang of it, ask your butcher for a shin of veal or a ham hock from which to make stock or to put straight into a soup with lentil or Scotch broth. Best of all, for something really powerful, put them all together with really strong vegetables such as celeriac and onions and you'll have an enviable winter warmer.

Fish and vegetable stock is a more delicate process, the latter because you want to extract the potent flavours of plants and merge them in liquid savour. If you have a pile of leftover vegetable stalks, skins and cuttings on your board ready to ditch, just give them a rinse, pop them in a pan and simmer for an hour. Leeks are a great ingredient because the mucus-like compound in their skins helps to set the stock naturally in the same way as does the marrow in bones. When it comes to making fish stock though, this can be a malodorous affair. But after a gluttonous seafood banquet, throw the heads, skin and tails and shellfish carapaces in a pan with some fennel, celery and a carrot to simmer gently for half an hour. This will result in a potent liquor for fish soup or *bouillabaisse*. Alternatively tell your fishmonger what you want and you'll be served up a terrifying bag of fish bits for stock.

One of the supposed secrets of the high priesthood of culinary skills is clarifying stock. And when you first achieve this transformation it is indeed a revelation, like seeing your bread dough rising for the first time. However, it isn't all that tricky. You let your stock chill, scrape off the congealed fat and put the stock back in a pan. Then whip up some egg whites (saving the yolks for mayonnaise or custard) to a froth, put them in the pan and slowly bring the stock to a gentle simmer, stirring slowly. The egg whites will gradually rise, lifting all the protein 'bits' in the stock to the surface. When this is a grey mass, skim it off, then finally pour the stock through a very fine sieve or a muslin cloth if you have one. You can improve this process by adding minced beef or even chicken to the egg in a blender first. Then add to the cold stock in the same way.

If necessary, once you've clarified your stock, you can strengthen it by continuing to simmer and reduce it. This increases the flavour and you can chill it again to serve as shots of consommé. If you need to add gelling agents, like aspic or gelatine, you can start playing around with some really fun cold starter dishes, suspending all sorts of things in the meaty jelly. Or just show off in winter by serving it up as a middle course with some delicate mushrooms like *girolles* or ceps floating in the steaming, clear, bronze liquid.

Most importantly, soup should be there just when you need it. And because it's freeze-able, you never have to run out of stock. We all deserve a spot of chicken soup when we are not well and it just doesn't work if it isn't home-made. Just the stock and some judiciously selected morsels of chicken does wonders for the spirits. And if your constitution can take it, you can heat up the stock with some rice and the juice of half a lemon so that it has a bit of a tang and you get the benefit of extra vitamin C. If you need some extra protein, break an egg into the soup and whisk it vigorously so you get little white strands. Whatever the indisposition, sleep will be induced and you will feel better when you awake.

If you do run short of fresh stock, quality bouillon mixes, stock cubes or cartons are great alternatives. In fact, you may even need some anyway if your stock hasn't got enough heart to it.

Ingredients

To start with, most soups benefit from some onions, chopped or sliced and cooked lightly in oil until they are soft and a golden colour. As always with onions, you'll find that they won't caramelise if you keep the lid on so the condensation runs back into the pan. At this stage, you can add garlic as you like it, freshly ground black pepper and a crumble of salt (not too much but it gives you an idea of whether you need to add extra flavour later). For a powerful onion soup, you can use different varieties and let them simmer for several hours until wholly caramelised.

For a hearty soup such as minestrone or Scotch broth, now you can really just chop up your ingredients, throw them in and let the whole thing simmer away. In creamier soups, for example celery, fennel, celeriac or broccoli, you need to make sure your ingredients have cooked properly before you blend them. This means adding them in the right order so they are all soft in texture at the end when you are ready to blend them. To get that extra luxurious quality, use a wooden spoon to press the soup through a sieve, which will take out all the unnecessary fibres.

Some starchy vegetables, for example potatoes, sweet potatoes, squashes and courgettes, make particularly creamy soups. Chop them small and boil them until soft, then add something braised or a little burned, such as fennel or chicory, for the surprise factor.

If you are going away on holiday and there are vegetables left in the fridge, cook them up, liquidise and freeze. You can put everything from lettuce leaves and radishes to aubergines and olives into soup.

Many soups benefit from having rice or pulses added. Rice can be added towards the end, just long enough for it to cook, or you can throw in a tin of cannellini or borlotti beans.

In the end, soup-making is an experiment with flavours and textures. If a hearty soup goes wrong, blend it, so leek and potato becomes vichyssoise. If you decide to add some texture to a creamier soup, everyone will love it all the same.

Even the more expert-sounding soups don't really demand much. Bisque in its finest form can be made from the leftovers of a fish stew or just ask your fishmonger for a selection of nice, cheap, sustainable fishy bits. Sometimes you might get some off-cuts too; something meaty and white like coley or pollack, mussels or prawns, and red mullet or salmon for colour. You want them filleted, so no bones. And if you're ever having crab or lobster at home, their remains make perfect stock with the addition of some vermouth.

Some soups may seem terribly complicated but there are easy ways to cheat. The autumnal *soupe aux marrons* is rather a trying experience, involving boiling up chestnuts in game stock and adding ground meat from a partridge or pheasant. The whole is then sieved and turned out with croûtons. But a lazy version might involve a tin of chestnut purée, mixed with fried aubergines (for the gamey flavour) and Parmesan. Once you've cooked the vegetables, you can just whizz them with the stock with the tin of purée and the Parmesan.

Though dishes like the Japanese *ramen* may be more of a main course, it's worth experimenting with. You need a pot of slowly steaming stock into which you can add any ingredients that will add a noticeable and distinctive flavour and aroma. So try grated ginger, lime juice, finely chopped garlic and chillies. Let them soak away for a while before adding your main ingredients. Find Asian varieties such as Chinese greens, pak choy, shredded pepper and spring onions. You can add seafood, such as prawns to give it some substance, and then, just at the end so they don't overcook, add some delicate mushrooms like *enoki* or *shiitake* and a handful of chopped coriander. And if you want more of a meal, then you can let some egg noodles soak in the hot broth at any stage.

For this and other lighter soups, you don't want to bully them with a heavy meat stock; you may even decide they need only water to allow other flavours to steal forth. This is the case with gazpacho, one soup where the vegetables are not peeled or cooked. You take a red and green pepper, a cucumber and some fresh plum tomatoes. The secret is to liquidise half of these ingredients with a heel of stale bread so you get some bite. With the addition of some garlic, herbs and dash of sherry vinegar or lemon juice, you get a thick, intense, chunky purée. Chop the rest of the ingredients very finely and spoon them in. Before you serve it chilled, you can drop some ice cubes into each bowl.

There are other soups that you'll want to be vibrant green and summery, such as watercress, lettuce or sorrel. They are perfect for hot summer lunches in the garden with a glass of ice-cold rosé. You want these to have their own energy and not lose that fresh crispness they have before being blended. The addition of cooked baby peas will maintain the verdant quality, though blending them raw and liquidising quickly will help to achieve this. But don't be disappointed by sorrel, which is sharp and immediate when a raw leaf but turns to grey slime when cooked. Find your own way.

As the cookery writer and chef Louis de Gouy wrote in 1949, 'Good soup is one of the prime ingredients of good living. For soup can do more to lift the spirits and stimulate the appetite than any other one dish.'

Garnishes

Soup benefits too from having something on top. And it looks great. Croûtons are the favourite. Little pieces of bread fried to a crisp in olive oil and added at the last minute give added mouth-feel, making the dish more interesting for the taste-buds. You can add some chopped garlic or chilli when cooking your croûtons for an extra bite. Or grate some cheese over your soup. Herbs such as parsley or mint bring a little vigour to smoother soups, or add a dollop of cream or yoghurt. Give your soup whatever it needs to make it the belle of the ball.

Soups adore a drop of booze. Think of them like cocktail floaters. So tomato soup loves vodka, celery craves a dash of anise, game a sly slug of brandy, and fish soup gets an elegant edge from vermouth. The stronger the soup, the stronger the flavour of the nip needs to be.

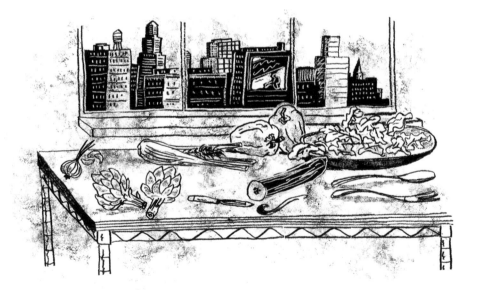

Shaking Up a Salad

The word salad describes so many variations on a theme. And yet in most homes and restaurants, the British salad is a surprisingly uninteresting performer. Amazingly, we still remain faithful to the lettuce, tomato, cucumber, pepper combination with some over-vinegary mustard dressing sloshing around – albeit we've moved beyond iceberg to radicchio.

And how disappointingly often salad appears in restaurants to make up plate space in a vain attempt to bring something to life or act as pointless garnish for an otherwise dreary dish. The point is that a salad should be poised and well-appointed, not an apology to cheer up the plate. It's something to prepare the palate if it is the prelude, the enhancing accompaniment to something bigger, or the liberating finale. Whatever the case, less is certainly more, and every element should be present for a reason. Nowhere does the right combination of flavours, textures and piquancy matter more. Too often, our salads are reluctant interlopers or just old hat.

For the new cook, you can really let your imagination loose on salads. You can compose anything you want, from recreating a standard hot dish as a salad to combining the bizarre and the sublime in hitherto unknown combinations.

Though you should follow your own counsel here, there are a few guidelines, common for a hotchpotch of ingredients in any dish, which will help you make a winning salad. The central advice is to not fall into the trap of bringing too many individuals who don't know each other to the party. You'll start to find cliques and resentment brewing between rival ingredients. The salad risks being over-run and disaster ensues. If this does happen, throw it all in a pot and make soup.

The leafy bits of your salad, whatever they are, must be lively and fresh. You can always tell when you are being given a salad thoughtlessly thrown together from one of those supermarket mix bags with a bottled dressing chucked over. You want something simple and elegantly dressed. Choose your own leaves, finding a balance of textures and flavours. Make sure they are washed and dried. And make your own dressing. It couldn't be easier.

It's worth preparing a salad carefully. It needs to be a vivifying dish, something to reinvigorate over-extended taste-buds or burst in on your palate with some new flavours. So when you are serving what are, in fact, raw vegetables, get rid of the unpalatable bits. Cores, skins, stalks and pips are easily removed. Don't forget too that any eligible salad item can be served on its own. Sometimes a judicious bowl of sliced cucumber or tomatoes, lightly dressed, is the best contender to a main course.

To accompany other dishes, you want something that both complements and differentiates. You need to think of giving your palate a rest but at the same time enlivening it. Frankly, the simpler the better. Nothing can really beat a very simple green salad with the lightest of oil dressings to cleanse the palate before cheese. Just a little curly lettuce or gem hearts, some chives and peeled cucumber.

Tomatoes can so often be tasteless and watery so you always need to use the best. If you aren't sure, then slice them and dress them with oil, salt, pepper and masses of garlic. Leave them to marinate like this for a while and when they are soft and enticing, tear up a big bunch of basil and you can just go on adding from there. Maybe some mozzarella, beetroot or sliced ripe avocado. If you can muster the energy, it's great to skin tomatoes and peppers for salad but equally when you want that solid, juicy crunch, keeping it on works too – another example of when you just have to run with your mood and desires.

For a salad to satisfy as a main dish, it has to have purpose and meaning. But you can really live the inspired cook dream here. The more unusual the combinations, the more interesting the results will be. There are so many combinations that make salad, from the classic Caesar with anchovies and croûtons to traditional Spanish house salad with white asparagus and tuna, olives and mayo, or the burning embers of a Thai salad with minced chicken, galangal, lemongrass and kaffir leaves. Potatoes served cold with chives, spring onions or sweet Spanish onions and mustardy mayonnaise can be marshalled into the front line with the addition of cold roast chicken or crisped back bacon. For a surprise hot potato salad, chop them with flat leaf parsley, and give them a French dressing and a sprinkling of toasted pine nuts.

Softer, cooked elements in a salad can tame the raw, crunchy ones. Doing this will also inspire you to use unusual ingredients in a salad, such as peas, cauliflower, mushrooms or even Brussels sprouts. Equally, for a hot salad, something crisply cold will bring it alive. Hot salads are an adventure in themselves and such a renewing alternative to the traditional way of eating meat or fish. There is something heavenly about the juices of a sliced pan-fried duck breast or brittle sardines against the crunch of crisp leaves, mopped up with crusty bread.

A salad tends to be low in carbohydrates, so if it is the main dish, add some croûtons fried in oil, or some lightly sautéed new potatoes.

Salads often benefit greatly from a few nuts or seeds, for example pine kernels, walnuts, pumpkin or sunflower seeds. But remember that nuts are always better slightly toasted as it releases their inner oils and intensifies the nuttiness. Sprinkling brown rice grains toasted in sesame oil is a sensational and surprising elbow in the ribs of most salads. For a softer crunch, sprouted seeds such as alfalfa or mung beans are a good alternative to leaves.

Cheese can elicit gasps of surprised pleasure when found hiding a salad. Try using crumbled feta, grated Parmesan, Pecorino or mozzarella *di bufala*, or sometimes consider less obvious contenders such as Roquefort or a crumbly Langres. Other cheeky additions, such as chopped soft-boiled eggs, capers, green peppercorns, anchovies and *cornichons*, all bring something quietly spectacular to the party.

Pulses and grains can make robust and stirring salads. Their strong foundation, without too much flavour, allows other ingredients to mingle, adding colour, textures and flavour. If you are looking for low-release carbs while dieting, then you won't go wrong with lentils with chopped peppers, lemon juice and artichoke hearts or even some goat cheese or buckwheat with peas, mint and asparagus.

The famous seventeenth-century gardener and diarist, John Evelyn, observed that he could 'by no means approve of the extravagant fancy of some, who tell us that a Fool is as fit to be the gatherer of Sallets as a wise man'. In putting together a salad he decides that 'every Plant must bear its part and they must fall into their places like the Notes in Music, and there must be nothing harsh or grating'. As with all of your cooking, salads must be balanced and sensible. Too many ingredients can kill the simplicity. Too little attention to detail will fail to bring it to life.

Dressings

Dressing is an unction, an emollient intended to coat the salad with a piquancy or overlay of flavour. But you have to learn not to over- or under-dress. In the same way as the wrong outfit can spoil a night out, an insipid, butch or nippy salad dressing can ruin the whole affair.

The basis of most dressings is a quality virgin olive oil; but you can use other oils, for example grapeseed, walnut or sesame, depending on the potency you seek. Melted butter is an alternative and poured still hot with lemon juice and masses of black pepper on a gem heart lettuce is simple perfection. Next, you need something to counter the oil, such as vinegar, freshly squeezed lemon or lime juice.

It's a good idea to have some different vinegars in the cupboard with which to experiment. There are countless vinegars to use, from wine and cider to tarragon and raspberry and everything between. They will give you room for exciting combinations, for example red wine vinegar pounded with anchovies, tarragon vinegar with English mustard and Worcestershire sauce, and simple, strong balsamic with the greenest olive oil.

Always taste the dressing before you toss the salad; if needs be, a squeeze of lemon juice, sprinkle of salt or splash of vinegar can revive but you can never return from overdoing it. Worcestershire sauce and mustard also add a little extra pizzazz to a blended dressing. Freshly ground pepper and a flaky salt, such as Maldon, is best, though be careful as each person might want to season their own salad.

There is no correct way to make a dressing. You may like to shake it up in a jar, mix it with a spoon or bash it together in your mortar. And the proportions of the ingredients will depend on your own taste. For that impact of freshness, don't dress the salad until the last minute, as the dressing immediately gets to work on the salad and the acids start to break down the lighter leaves. So if you want to keep the leftovers, then serve it in a jug or bowl with a gorgeous spoon and let people dress it on the plate.

Don't forget that a dressing for salad dishes based on Asian ingredients and flavours will need some different ingredients. Pound some toasted cashews or peanuts and sesame seeds using your pestle and mortar. Add grated ginger, chilli powder, lime juice or rice vinegar, garlic, sesame oil or a dribble of fish sauce. Add handfuls of freshly chopped coriander at the end. For North African salads, such as *babaganoush* made from cooked bulgur wheat, you might want to think of using spices such as cinnamon or cumin and fresh green herbs.

Coming out of Its Shell

If you have ever been to the French Riviera, or any coastal resorts in the world where the rich idle away their hours in shimmering white linens, you will have eaten in those quayside restaurants serving towers of shellfish – all limbs, shells, claws and tendrils. The places that have water tanks full of your dinner swimming around, ready for you to select your victim. You may have looked at the icy marble slabs of your local fish market, overloaded with sleepy crustaceans and molluscs, and wanted to pluck up the courage to take some home for supper.

Like many kinds of food, shellfish has acquired a rarefied reputation.

Partly this is because it tends to be expensive and hard to find. In fact, like most seafood, we have over-harvested shellfish, but more significantly we have polluted its natural habitat so much that it only thrives in certain places. And because this has increased the demand for the best quality, they are often immediately exported to the markets where they fetch the highest prices. Scottish crustaceans and molluscs are often whisked away to Paris and Barcelona before most locals can get their hands on them.

First let's understand exactly what we are dealing with. There are two kinds of shellfish: crustaceans and molluscs. The first are mostly seafaring invertebrates with tough external carapaces and include lobster, crab, langoustine, crawfish, prawn and shrimp. The second are the creatures that live in shells and are mostly bivalves, that is they have two halves to their homes, like oysters, mussels, scallops and clams. Strangely, although they have no shells, squid and octopus are also technically molluscs. Those very British seaside treats like cockles, winkles and whelks are another family of molluscs again but it's the first two we'll have most dealings with.

Although it looks tricky, mostly shellfish doesn't require much cooking. So for someone expanding their cooking repertoire, it's a way of impressing friends with your new-found culinary talent. The most important thing is freshness and that's partly the reason why you tend to only find them at their best in places next to the coast, or from quality fishmongers inland whose customers are prepared to pay a premium for them.

Most shellfish needs to be alive when you buy it fresh, so you are looking for shiny shells and some movement in the limbs (thankfully crustaceans do go a bit sleepy on ice); for molluscs, it's essential that the valves still work, so that their shells still open and close up until the point that you cook them. Go with your instinct and never buy shellfish that looks dead, has broken shells, is sitting in pools of opaque water or if it just looks generally unappetising.

Cooking all fresh shellfish is fairly simple but a little gruesome, as they are best cooked alive. Most crustaceans are best plunged into a large pan of boiling water, just long enough to cook the flesh through – often only a few minutes. With molluscs you can also steam them in a sealed pan, which will open the valves. If a mollusc shell is open before cooking or doesn't open when cooked, bin it.

The big boys are quite a handful. You need to be fairly hardened to be boiling a crab or lobster alive and confident with a knife once they are out of the pan. For the novice it would be more sensible to start with something manageable and not too expensive that won't nip and is easy to shell. Something smaller, for example langoustines or Dublin Bay prawns, are winners on all levels. They taste supreme when their firm flesh is just out of the water, they look outstanding with their pink shells, and served simply with lemon, bread and home-made mayonnaise, they are unbeatable. Sitting there in the sun, picking out the flesh, you will never wonder again at the sophistication of it all.

To get you started, here are some suggestions for cooking shellfish that will help you build know-how and confidence.

Lobster

Lobsters require careful handling as their pincers can literally break your finger. Usually they are bound with a rubber band to stop them eating each other, but watch how your fishmonger handles them, always picking up the creature from its body with its head facing away from you. There are different ways to cook them and some believe that it is more humane to put them in the freezer for an hour to slow down their metabolism. But in truth these creatures cannot be compared to mammals and their physiology is mostly a nervous and digestive system, so in effect, you can't really kill them, just close down one of those elements.

Either way, as quick as you can, put them in the biggest pan of salted boiling water you can find. Bring it back to the boil and for an average lobster (about half a kilo) you need to time it for about 15 minutes. When it's ready to come out, your deep blue lobster will have turned an exotic pink. Leave it to cool and then take a sharp knife and, with the head facing you this time, cut halfway down the middle from the head to the tail. When it's open, remove the unattractive looking bits, which are essentially the stomach, liver and sometimes some eggs (for aficionados these latter bits can be delicacies but if you are unsure, stick to the meat). Break off the claws, cut them open and remove the flesh.

Crab

The arguments go on, but for some reason it is felt that because crabs take longer to cook and sometimes shed their limbs, killing them before you boil them is more humane. It's quite simple. You turn the creature on its back and at the back of the shell there is a small flap over a hole. Push a screwdriver through the hole and tap it through to the other side of the shell with a little tug. Then turn the crab over and let the water drain out. Pop it into the salted boiling water for about twenty minutes per kilo and add five minutes for every 500 grammes above that.

Preparing them for cooking is more complicated than lobster, which is frankly why I only ever eat crab in restaurants, but if you've got this far, let the crab cool, wash it off and remove the claws. You can crack those and remove the flesh. For the main body, it's best to hold the body head down and insert your thumbs, removing the underside. As with lobster, you will expose the stomach, which can be removed. Once that is done you can remove the flesh. Both the white and rich brown meat can be spooned out. Incidentally, if you prefer the white meat you should ask your fishmonger for male or cock crabs, as they have more.

Langoustines (Dublin Bay Prawns), Prawns and Brown Shrimp

Langoustines or prawns are easier to prepare and cook than their bigger relatives but pretty much the same rules apply. Langoustines (also known as Dublin Bay prawns) are actually related to lobsters; prawns are a different family amongst which are the deep-water prawn or Northern shrimp, spot shrimp, pink shrimp, white shrimp, brown shrimp and king prawn.

A note of caution on environmental concerns: all cold-water prawns, such as those farmed in Iceland, are fine to eat but you should avoid exotic tiger prawns, which are mostly farmed in the mangroves of South-East Asia in the most unsustainable and often destructive ways. Madagascar and Ecuador are the only countries that have made strides towards ensuring their tiger prawn farming techniques are sustainable and ethical. Look out for them, but do ask your fishmonger about the provenance of what you are buying.

Smaller shellfish are usually frozen at sea, so you will only rarely find them completely fresh. Larger prawns can be grilled with melted butter or thrown straight into a fish soup. The skins of the smaller varieties, such as brown shrimps, when cooked, can sometimes be eaten with the flesh.

Oysters

Though they are now perceived to be the food of luxury, oysters were the staple diet of the working classes throughout history. Geologists have found pre-ice age archipelagos built on the shingle of billions of oyster shells, and in the eighteenth century they were the food of the poor. They were used in French Creole cooking, and in England they were added to steak and kidney pudding. However, the habit of eating them raw was not widespread until more recently.

There is nothing like a little shot of the sea with a crisp white wine, and oysters are not difficult to produce for a meal at home. Like all shellfish, freshness is the key and you need to make sure the shell is working. Opening or 'shucking' oysters is the tricky bit and if you aren't experienced it can get messy – and frustrating – with bits of shell everywhere. A solution is to pop them in the freezer for a few hours. There they will naturally open and you can just remove the top shell, then leave them for an hour while they come back up to the right temperature for eating. Fresh and lovely, serve them with bread, lemon juice and Tabasco for those who do.

You can grill or roast oysters too. You might want to wash the outside of the shells, taking care not to cut yourself, then put them whole under the grill or in the oven, covered with a sheet of foil to prevent them burning (this also works on a barbecue). After about five minutes, their shells will automatically start opening and the oysters can be extracted. Grilled oysters with a little cream, chopped tarragon, butter and Parmesan on toast are astonishing.

Mussels, Cockles and Clams

Check that the shells are closed and clean them well. The traditional French way of cooking mussels *marinières* with onions, celery, flat leaf parsley and a little white wine seems to extract the best from these fishy wonders without imposing too much upon them. There are many other additions and different sauces – the addition of a little curry, cream or even Roquefort cheese can create a sumptuous feast. And of course, the Belgians love them with *frîtes* and lightly chilled Alsace Pinot Noir.

Clams and cockles can be treated in the same way, though razor clams, which are the long comb-shaped variety, are a little more fleshy and flourish on a plate with garlic, lemon juice and a tomato or cream sauce. The smaller, round clams and cockles can be cooked in a little oil, coriander and lemon juice in a pan with the lid on. The shells will open and you can serve them as they are, licking their juices from the shells.

Scallops

These molluscs are successful in the waters around Britain and have a firm texture and meaty flavours. You should always buy hand-dived King scallops because the alternative are caught by dredging, which just scours the sea floor and destroys anything else that exists there. 'Queenies' and Princess scallops are also available, with various debates about farming, dredging and sustainability. Make your choices knowledgeably and never buy them if they have been slopping in water at the fishmonger.

Always acquire them in the shell; the experience will be entirely more satisfactory. Hold the scallop in your hand with the flat side up. Take a blunt table knife and slip it between the shell to open up the valve. This will reveal a perky white body with the orange roe. Around that is a brown 'skirt' which can be removed along with any other bits. Basically you want to end up with the round white scallop and its orange roe in the shell. At this point you can decide whether to grill it in the shell or remove it to pan-fry. A favourite for scallops is to have them with something like bacon or chorizo – the flavour responds well. The standard French favourite is *Coquilles St Jacques*, where they are removed from the shell, sautéed with onion, white wine, parsley and put back in the shell to be grilled with Parmesan.

Roast Dinners

Sometimes you can come home from your local supermarket with a duck, put it in the oven and leave it for two hours without looking at it once. It will emerged crisp-skinned, with perfectly moist flesh – a flavoursome accident which you can never repeat. That sometimes is just the way with roasting. For all the things you can do to prepare meat and poultry for cooking, sometimes nothing makes any difference at all and your expensive joint ends up looking like a dried up leather satchel or a deep-fried alien. At other times, you catch the timing just right and it's a juicy triumph for all to enjoy.

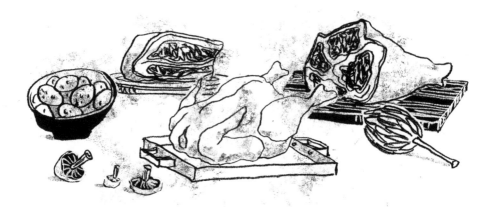

Like all kinds of cooking, roasting is about trial and error. But to start with there are some approaches, without getting too complicated, that will build your confidence and produce some pretty impressive results.

As always, you need to study what you are about to cook to understand what it will need. Birds come from different backgrounds and with varying characteristics. The flesh of beasts also has different qualities: some joints will be light, others need long and slow roasting to break down the fibres in the meat. Pork always has a tendency to dry out because the meat is so dense, so you need to be careful not to overcook it. In terms of what you want to add to accompany the roast, it will depend on what you have in the cupboard or fridge or how much you need to spice it up.

There are three basic steps to roasting. First you need a period of very high heat, which crisps up the outside of the flesh or the skin of a bird; then a steady cooking at a lower heat; finally allowing the bird or joint to 'rest' out of the oven, usually covered.

Once it is prepared, place the joint or bird in a roasting tin or a terracotta cooking dish and start it off in the hottest oven – say 250 degrees centigrade – you want to get the outside starting to crisp up and sizzle. This should be for about a quarter of the cooking time, which will depend on its size. You can find specific cooking times for meat and poultry in your favourite recipe books. For meat that risks drying out, at this stage add a little water (or better, wine) to the bottom of the roasting tin and continue to do so throughout cooking, which keeps the whole thing succulent.

After the initial blast, turn down the heat to a reasonable 190–200 degrees celcius and let it cook steadily. Lay some foil over the top if you're worried about it burning or drying out. When a bird is overcooked the skin will have stretched taut across the leg and breast, which isn't the outcome you're looking for, so keep an eye on it. Also remember that when you take anything out of the oven and cover it in foil, it will continue to cook.

The important thing throughout roasting is to ensure you retain the moisture. You can achieve this by basting throughout cooking but it's a tiresome process, you lose the heat of the oven when you open the door so it takes longer to cook, and it doesn't really make much of a difference on anything bigger than a rack of lamb or a pheasant. It's generally easier to create the moisture you need in other ways. However, if you are using a turkey baster, which looks like a big syringe, then you need to create some incisions in the flesh and make sure you are actually squeezing the liquid into the meat.

Whatever you do, don't throw away any juices or residue at the bottom of the cooking dish. Even if it seems dried up or burnt, a bit of coaxing from some boiling water and a vigorous scraping with your wooden spoon will release some dark gravy bits which soften with liquid (some aromatic booze like sherry or port can make a rather special addition here) and simmer away.

Other than this, you can place a wire grill at the bottom of the roasting pan, covered or open, with steaming liquid below. But by far the easiest method is to keep adding stock, wine or water at the base of whatever you're cooking. As this evaporates, the flesh will absorb it, with whatever flavours you have added. If you want the whole joint or bird to be crisp, you can turn it round halfway.

Roasting Birds

You need to be careful that a bird isn't undercooked, doesn't dry out and is assisted to retain whatever natural flavours it has. Sometimes chickens come large on the breast front, while others have legs like rugby players. These need more care because they don't cook evenly. If you are lucky enough to be able to get one that has lived long enough to have evenly dispersed yellowing fat (hard to find outside France), it will be easy enough to cook. Generally breasts cook more quickly and can have a tendency to dry out if they are not given the right support through the roasting process.

Turkeys tend to defy even the best cooks. They are wayward and highly individual. What works once seldom does so again. In fact, sometimes the less you do to a turkey, the better. Your favourite cooks will describe what you need to do, some prescribing cooking upside down or end-up, others larding, buttering or covering in foil. Frankly, they are overweight and ungainly in life and mostly unrewarding on the plate.

For very small birds like pigeon, quail or small game birds, which can be more trouble than the results you get, you can cook them in a heavy-lidded pot or, even better, use your sharp knife to slice down the breast bone and cut out the breast fillets, then pan-fry them in butter.

Whatever and however you plan, you have to think about what kinds of flavours you want to impart. A gently fragrant herb, such as tarragon or oregano, can be put inside the bird or underneath as it cooks. But you could also rub rosemary leaves or sage into the skin, or put bay leaves inside or underneath it. Garlic pressed into small incisions all over the flesh of the bird will bring out rich aromas, and very thin slivers of lemon drizzled with honey will add a nutty stickiness on the skin. Pretty much anything you want to coat, smear or massage on to your chicken will work. Sometimes the most effective is just butter and salt.

Some birds respond very well to the addition of fruit during cooking. The sweetness can cut through strong flavours and absorb too much cloying fat. Cherries have always been a traditional Normandy accompaniment to duck, prunes to pheasant, chestnuts with chicken, partridge with grapes. Perhaps introducing cranberries to a turkey earlier in the relationship might bring something more interesting to that combination. My personal favourite with duck is to smear marmalade all over the bird in the last 20 minutes so that it caramelises the skin and creates a citrusy bite. As with all cooking, be bold. Add your own ideas, cover the bird in whatever you like to see if it will work. The worst that can happen is that it doesn't and you have to take it off the skin. It's hard to completely ruin poultry and game during cooking unless you entirely cremate it. With a bit of imagination, you can always find some way of salvaging a meal.

You can also roast a bird upside down. I'm not sure that it works for a turkey, which you just need to keep moist any way possible. But for a chicken or duck it can have surprisingly positive results, especially if you want to leave the bird on for a few hours at a low temperature. That is breaking the rules we've just agreed, of course, but then that's what cooking is all about.

Stuffing birds is a mixed bag. It's an ancient custom and in really extravagant feasts, birds were stuffed with the most exotic ingredients – including other birds and meats, dried fruits and nuts. More recently and closer to home, people went for stuffing when times were hard because it added vital ballast to the meal. As with all cooking, you can do anything you like and some recipes really go to town. But there are two reasons to be cautious. First, if you are using something like sausage meat, it risks being undercooked inside the bird. Second, a bird's skeleton offers the perfect cooking scaffold and so stuffing does interrupt the cooking time because you are filling the cavity where all the heat circulates and spreads throughout the flesh. In addition, leaving this cavity empty can keep a bird moister.

You could experiment with a few strong-tasting vegetables such as sliced onions or celery in the cavity, or put them under the bird so that they cook in the juices. Alternatively, if you love stuffing, just cook it separately and add it to the whole dish before serving. Lots of Italian and French dishes require stuffing boned birds (sometimes with other smaller birds). This sounds more difficult than it is and involves starting with the wings and gradually turning the bird inside out, leaving the bones aside for making stock. The bird can then be stuffed and trussed. But to be honest, less is more. The bony scaffolding of a bird is the perfect structure to allow things to cook just nicely and the juices to flow with minimum fuss.

A word to the wise: make sure you remove the giblets, which are the inside bits of a bird – liver, heart and neck – and are usually found in plastic bags inside a well-sourced bird. They are essential for making gravy but the aroma of melted plastic inside your bird isn't a nice way to start a meal.

Larding a bird is another way of adding flavour and moisture. It involves taking pieces of pork fat and stringing them through the flesh of a bird or creating incisions and pushing the fat in. For anything small, it can interfere with delicate flavours but if you have the patience, it can also make a big turkey juicier. Domestic goose and duck, which are already very fatty, wouldn't need this, but adding some bacon to a pheasant or wrapping a partridge in ham or the thick Italian bacon called *pancetta* can help to balance the strong flavours of the game and keep the bird juicy.

When you think your bird is done, cut into it where the leg meets the body. If the juices run clear, it's ready. Now you can do one of two things. With bigger birds, either carve at the table or, to make it go further, remove the meat from the bones – it should be falling off – and cut your crisp skin into bites for those who like it (eat some with your fingers while no-one is looking). With game birds, there is a fashion to serve them whole and with slightly pinker flesh. Personally, while bloody steak meat works, undercooked birds are a bore, unless they are very young, tender baby woodpigeon. Just give your guests a well-cooked, moist fowl and permission to tear at it with their fingers.

Roasting Meat

Meat pretty much requires you to observe the same general rules as birds. You need to think about what you want to end up with: something moist with plenty of mouth-filling flavour and texture. Again, the animals we eat have different characteristics so you need look at the flesh and decide where to start. Cattle and sheep have more active lives gambolling around the fields and moorlands and benefit from a high ingestion of fresh grass, whereas pigs do a lot of snuffling and rooting around for a different diet with much less activity. Inevitably the results show in the characteristics of the animal's flesh, and it's one of the reasons to always go for the finest-bred, organic, free-range meat you can. It will be easier to cook and the results will win the highest praise.

The most common roast dinner in Britain other than chicken is beef. It's the mainstay of Sundays and is so often destroyed by being poorly cooked. There is always a fear of undercooking when it comes to beef, which inevitably means it turns up at the table overcooked. The reason for this is that the flesh is quite thickly grained and marbled with fat so it conducts heat relatively quickly – at least more so than other flesh. But this also means that it loses heat quickly, so we often end up with a nicely pink and bloody but cold beef joint by the time it hits the table. So more than any other roast, cooking beef needs to be done as near the eating time as you can. Better to keep people waiting a bit for sizzling but immaculately pink roast than turning out something brown and leathery.

A leg of lamb is in the interesting position of having lots of complex elements but with very tender flesh at the thigh. We tend to like it pink but that makes it more difficult to ensure it is well cooked across the whole joint. In fact, mutton is a safer bet. The meat is older and richer in flavour and it roasts more evenly, giving you a more sophisticated flavour on the plate. A shoulder joint is actually far more satisfying to cook and the rewards are greater in my book. You can literally throw it into the oven with some herbs, potatoes and vegetables and it will cook itself slowly for hours. When it emerges, you will have a fine meal to feed your friends and family. But beware if you have a delicate constitution, as sheep fat is generally hard to digest and may play havoc with your natural balances.

Pork is made for roasting. The thick layer of fat and the pork rind on the outside keeps the moisture soaking into the meat, which is itself quite lean. Most joints are rolled for you by a butcher but you will also find belly pork, which has less meat but benefits from long, extensive roasting; a rack of pork with its ribs and chops is a stunning cut to cook for a special occasion. Although you should always leave any meat out for a while before cooking, so that it comes up to room temperature, pork responds well to being left out overnight. Rubbing salt into pork rind which has been scored criss-cross with a knife will produce the most enticing crackling. For those worried about the fat intake, if you can, separate the rind, cut away some fat and place some seasonings and herbs under the skin before putting the rind back in place.

Gammon joints or hams have the added value of providing many lunches and dinners afterwards. You do need to buy something worthwhile though because most mass-produced gammon has had water added and can even sometimes be made up from reconstituted 'bits' of meat. Boil gammon in something with sugar in it, for example cider, beer or even cola, which is a dish from the deep south of America recommended by Nigella Lawson. This lends a dark richness to the meat which can be finished off with a mustardy or honey crust before serving.

Adding flavours and accompanying ingredients to meat joints for roasting can have a powerful impact, particularly with lamb and pork. They both respond to having strong, sweet spices, fruits and herbs pushed into their flesh and fatty seams. You can make incisions with a knife and cut along the grain of the meat or, if you have a rolled joint from the butcher, ask him for some extra ties. Unroll the joint, and layer and coat the folds and fleshy crevices with a pounded paste of titillating ingredients. You can use almost anything and it's fun to experiment all the time. In your mortar, throw one or two of your key seeds or spices, some garlic, olive oil, lemon juice and grated zest and crush them with the pestle, pounding it all to a sticky, smelly, sweet paste.

With lamb, you can add anchovies, which lose all their fishiness but lend the meat a potent depth while it cooks. Pork loves dried fruits such as apricots, which can be placed under the skin. Balsamic vinegar, soy or Worcestershire sauces always give a vote of flavour to lamb, infusing the meat with dark, sweet aromas. Really, the advice must be to let your creative juices flow. Look to see what you have in the fridge and in your cupboards and then use your innovative skills to try something out. As long as you don't overcook meat, you can pretty much do anything and still be able to rescue it if you're worried that it didn't work.

The only game meat you are likely to cook at this stage will be venison or rabbit. If you are lucky enough to get hold of a haunch of venison, then mash up juniper berries, redcurrants (or a similar fruit) with garlic, oil and honey, salt and pepper and make sure the whole is sufficiently covered so that as you cook it slowly, those odours fill the kitchen. Have a bottle of port or red wine at hand to slosh over it periodically. Rabbit actually responds better to stewing but can be roasted after being jointed, which means taking apart the limbs and cutting the rabbit into pieces. It goes well with prunes and, famously, Hermitage wine.

Stews

There are two ways of cooking meat, birds or fish in a pot: in bits or whole. The former is known as a stew or 'casserole' (like so many dishes, this is named after the type of dish in which it is cooked) and the latter comes in many guises, often called a pot-roast. They can both be cooked either on the hob or in the oven. Though purists might argue the case, every cooking appliance is different and no-one better than you knows how the one in your kitchen works.

Stews are generally made using smaller pieces of your main ingredients with additional vegetables and pulses. They are a wholesome way of using cheaper cuts because the slow cooking makes the least appetising meat tender and succulent. Fish doesn't much like being submerged in hot liquid for too long as it dries out, so it needs to be cooked more quickly. Stews are one of the best ways to cook game, as the richness really evolves as it simmers, imbuing the whole dish with aromatic odours and sumptuous flavours.

You will also hear the expression pot-roasting, particularly in America, but this is somewhat of a misnomer as it is effectively the same as a stew, except you are generally cooking a whole bird or piece of meat. It works by the same principle as the French dish *pot-au-feu* or *poule au pot* in which the meat or bird is cooked in a large, heavy-lidded pot or a clay *marmite* on the hob.

The most useful aspect to stews and anything cooked in this way is that for the newcomer to cookery, it's possibly one of the easiest ways to succeed in creating what is essentially quite a complex combination of flavours and textures. It's not difficult to impress yourself and guests with a well-made stew or casserole. And because you can make it days before (it's better if you do), it takes all the stress out of being a new cook.

The cooking is simple and the preparation is even easier: an example of the 'chop it up and chuck it in' school. By understanding what your dish needs at the beginning in terms of the balance of flavours, adding the right seasoning and herbs, the ingredients will do it all for you. All you need is one of the attributes of an experienced cook: patience. Open the lid many hours later and the most powerful, sumptuous dish will present itself to you, with meat falling apart and abundant flavours emerging from the steaming liquid.

In the previous chapter we looked at how to choose what sort of cut of meat or ingredients you might want to use for a stew. Personally I don't believe in using any cuts I wouldn't eat normally. Just think of those stews at school or in staff canteens, with knobbly bits of chewy gristle. Why risk it? Just buy something decent that you can be sure will surface from the pot with robust and joyful confidence. A shin of beef cut up, or mutton, a much underused meat, which is only lamb that has reached eight months of age, has bags of flavour and is perfect for stews.

The first thing is to brown the meat, which is known as braising. As we've explained before, this starts a caramelisation process going which just adds some interesting flavours to the pot. Next you probably want to fry some onions and garlic in there, which helps with producing a body in the liquor. As with all herbs, just decide which ones you want to use, but at this stage you are looking for something woody like bay leaves, thyme or rosemary. Some peppercorns and sea salt (though be careful how much salt you add at this stage, it's better to be safe and season it once the stew is finished) and, of course, something from the wine rack will add potential to your concoction.

Whatever vegetables you want to use can be added now. Go for the favourites like carrots, turnip, swede and leek but also try some of your new acquaintances. Celeriac, fennel, kohl rabi and even beetroot are happy stewing mates.

When your dish is done and before serving, you can decide to freshen up the flavours with some other vegetables or fill it out with potatoes, rice, pasta or even dumplings. The introduction of greens like kale or *cavolo nero* before serving gives the stew new life. You can even serve it on a large croûton toasted in extra virgin olive oil, or a plate of wilted spinach. The choice is yours.

Pot roasting follows pretty much the same principle and you will find dishes from all over the world that involve braising a piece of meat and introducing differing amounts of liquids to cook it off, from boiling pork slowly in milk and sweet spices to cooking beef in a mixture of vinegar and wine.

When you pot-roast a chicken you follow exactly the same procedure as making a stew. When it's done, the best thing is to remove the carcass and add fresh vegetables, potatoes, rice or pulses. Cook them in the stock and return the meat to the pot, off the bone, and serve. Not a shred of the chicken, or its flavours, is lost. It's a different way to eat chicken and is perfect if you want a hearty, warming, soupy dish that lasts for days or can feed a multitude.

Fishing Around

Cooking fish couldn't really be easier. Because the flesh of fish is much less complex than meat, you can grill, fry, bake, roast and marinade most fish ready for the table in a matter of minutes. Once you've decided whether you are eating it whole, in pieces or skinned and filleted, cooking is mostly about maintaining the freshest taste, keeping the flesh firm and moist and, if you want to eat the skin, making sure it's nice and crispy.

For most skinned and filleted white sea fish, the easiest option is to bake it or fry it gently in oil or butter in your pan, with the addition of little else except perhaps a little white wine, seasoning and some herbs. This sounds like a generalisation and the scope is really endless but it's important to retain the sea flavour of fish while ensuring you don't overwhelm it with too much of anything else.

Conversely, freshwater fish, such as eel, pike, carp and perch, tend to have a rather rough and ready, muddy flavour which you need to finesse. A rich cheese sauce helps pike along, or you can use it for fishcakes with lots of dill and pepper. For me, eel is the unrepentant serving wench of the fish world and I would be wary of serving it if you are entertaining, but it can be civilised a bit with a strong tomato and wine sauce. Frankly, despite attempts by popular pundits to tell you how good it is, eel will never come to my table. Each to their own.

However you are cooking fish, you need to make sure it doesn't dry out, so it needs lots of moisture, and if you are putting it under the grill or baking it, keep a constant eye on it as the turning point for it to dry out is easily missed. Overall, the advice I would give with fish is not to cook it until absolutely the last moment you need to.

Marinating fish is a godsend, particularly if you find yourself with fresh fish you are not going to use immediately and which is already too late to freeze. It's simply the impact of the acid of citrus juice or the sugary enzymes of fruit such as pineapple or papaya (for Indonesian or Asian flavours) breaking down the flesh and imbuing it with the flavours of the marinade. Start with either one of the ingredients above and, depending on the end result you want, add some simple layers of flavour. The simplest marinade to start with mixes lemon juice, olive oil, seasoning and a dried herb such as fenugreek or fresh coriander. You can introduce garlic or wine, if you want to build stronger flavours. It's tempting to want to use the juices once the fish has done and you are ready to cook it but make sure you taste it first as there can be quite a transformation. Fish can last a day or two like this but if you are marinating to eat the fish raw, as with Mexican *ceviche*, discard the marinade.

There was a time when every cook had a fish kettle, usually for poaching a salmon. But then came the late-departed television chef, Keith Floyd, and he showed us how to bake a salmon wrapped in layers of wet newspaper in the oven. As you remove the paper, the

skin comes off and a perfectly pink whole fish is revealed, ready for the slices of cucumber to garnish it for a cold buffet. An alternative to this, which can be used for any fish, is to oven cook your fish in a kitchen foil parcel. This keeps all the liquid in and effectively steams the flesh, retaining the flavours of your herbs or stuffing. Cooking whole fish embedded in salt has a similar effect and looks incredibly impressive when brought to the table. But you have to be wary of allowing the salt to make contact with the flesh.

Fish skin is important. Unlike vegetables and fruit, the skin of fish is packed with lovely oils called Omega 3. There have been countless studies that seem to show that these sustain brain power, reduce aggression and generally keep you limber. So you want to eat fishy skin if possible. But it can be a bit hard to stomach if it isn't well cooked, so my advice is to always crisp it up a bit. You can drizzle on some soy sauce or balsamic vinegar to give it a richer taste.

Cooking a whole fish, particularly if it's so fresh it practically jumped from the sea on to your plate, will always bring the best results. You almost have to do nothing to it at all. Keep the head and tail on because it looks nicer, and if it's so long you can't get it in the oven, it's better to cook it in two halves, reuniting them at the table, than hacking away at the head and tail, which always ends in a dog's breakfast. Scoring along the skin helps because, unsurprisingly, it's impervious to liquid, so doing this allows all the flavours you add to mingle and the heat to circulate quickly. As described above, lay your fish out on a sheet of foil and, if you like, stuff something in the cavity that will infuse the fish with the aromas you want. Fennel and fresh herbs such as coriander and dill work for this, as do onions and lemon rind. Well-appointed spices come into their own here, sprinkled on the skin. Cinnamon, ground ginger, cumin or caraway seeds all give off a powerful scent which will assault the senses, when the fish is unwrapped.

Serving fish and shellfish together makes for a posh dish. Think prawns with white fish fillets or cooking a whole wild sea trout in season and serving it with clams.

Among the less obvious fish to cook, happily locally caught and sustainable, fresh mackerel has made a comeback in recent years. Being an oily fish it's terribly healthy, though has an unfortunate propensity to return on your breath, so you need to make sure you eat it with something that is acidic enough to break down those fish oils. Rather notoriously, mackerel is outrageously companionable with rhubarb. Who would have thought of that? It has rather thick skin, so slice into it or fry it to a crisp.

Sardines have moved on a long way from their standard British performance on toast at high tea and nowadays you can buy the French varieties, which are somewhat more exotic and better prepared before being tinned. You can do something inspired with fresh sardines, but honestly, nothing is nicer than eating them grilled over a campfire with lots of lemon and fresh bread and butter. In fact, just go into the garden or nearest park and light up for the sake of it.

Squid and octopus look quite scary when you see them hiding among the other fish in the ice, with their eyes boggling. But they are a joy to eat, with that meatiness, and respond well to strong, smoky flavours and textures such as roasted garlic, heavy tomato purée and sausages such as chorizo or salami and black pudding. Squid, most commonly served in those battered rings from Nice to Skegness, is quick to flash or stir-fry. You will have seen it appearing with criss-cross scores across the soft side of the skin, which helps it cook quickly and absorb more of the flavours. But beware, cooking it for too long makes it tough.

Octopus has much thicker tentacles and needs to be slowly cooked in a casserole or stew. If you're having a barbecue, go Mediterranean and hang out the octopus whole to dry out, then put it on the charcoal grill to cook. With a glass of cold wine, close your eyes and you'll be back in the Cyclades.

If you have some nice sustainable white fish fillets, such as wrasse, or even something like river cobbler, which are often in the supermarkets, then a quick triumph is to slice them into thin strips and dip in egg and then the breadcrumbs you've been keeping in the freezer: goujons with a blob of home-made mayonnaise. Everyone will be impressed – if you haven't eaten them all before they get to the table.

Salmon and trout follow pretty much the same rules. If you're cooking fillets, they need a bit of flavour, but you can grill or pan-fry them and then add the frills as you like.

Fish Stew

This is worth a separate explanation because it is such an unrivalled dish. Though technically it doesn't fall into the same category as meat stews, you are essentially cooking something in its own juices in a big pot. And because a standard fish stew is such a useful addition to the cook's repertoire, it's useful to have a version up your sleeve and doesn't need much else but bread and wine.

Like all stews, you need balance: rich liquid and a range of potent flavours steaming from your pot. But unlike meat, fish cooks quickly so you don't want it stewing for hours. For a quick fish stock, the easiest thing is to quickly boil up some vegetables with the remains of any shellfish and fish heads and tails. The fishmonger will sell you these or you can use the bits from the fish you are about to prepare and make the stock on the spot.

In terms of what to use, please yourself. Some people like oily fish like salmon and mackerel in a fish stew, others find it too cloying. I'd go for a mix and see which ones you like best. Be aware, as always, of what is sustainable. I know I mention this a lot but fishing policy internationally is so screwed up we all have to do our bit to make sure these other fish get used. Pollock, megrim and coley are just as good as any of their more obvious cousins, and oily fish, such as sardines and herring, are also enjoying a bit of a recovery in UK waters. Shellfish can be hand-gathered instead of dredging, and herbivorous fish like carp, tilapia, and barramundi are doing well in freshwater ponds.

Start by making a spicy tomato sauce. Fry garlic in extra virgin oil, add turmeric, cayenne pepper, green peppercorns and when sizzling, add two tins of plum tomatoes. Reduce this lot until it's a thickish, dark red paste, add the stock and a bottle of decent white wine. You should be looking at a vat of winey, steaming red liquor. Add two sliced fennel bulbs and simmer.

While it's simmering, cut up your chunks of fish. Grill anything with skin, that side up, with soy sauce until very crispy. If you are using shellfish like mussels or clams, beard and scrub as described in the previous section, and have some fresh langoustines at the ready (their wispy limbs add something to the mix).

Now add everything gradually. First the white fish to cook in the sauce and then the squid and the shellfish. When that's done, add the oily fish and some parsley. Take it bubbling to the table and mop up with large chunks of bread spread generously with a fresh *salsa verde* of coriander, tarragon, basil, lemon juice, olive oil, garlic, sea salt and fresh broken pepper.

Any leftovers can be blended and sieved to make a potent bisque for Sunday supper.

Fish Pie

When the weather is rough and you need some home comfort, fish pie is the best. You can really use any combination of pink or white fish with some prawns. Cook the fish in a bit of butter and flake it into the bottom of a pie dish with the prawns. Toast some almonds (soak them, take the skin off and split them) or pine nuts in what's left of the fishy butter. Next hard-boil four eggs (I usually put them into the pot with the potatoes) and chop them into the dish. Then cook some peas – more than you think you'll need – it makes a more complete dish. Some people use leeks but they have a rather glutinous effect on the pie. Next whisk up some light béchamel sauce and pour it over – sufficient to cohere the whole, and top it off with creamy mashed potato. Fifteen minutes in the oven and finished off under the grill should do it.

Risking a Risotto

There is no point pretending that making the finest risotto doesn't require experience and ultimately a very special art. But like so many dishes it has developed a mystique which prevents people from having a go at what is, in fact, a comparatively easy dish to cook, providing you follow a few rules. There is only one way to build the knowledge you'll need to satisfy your most fussy Italian friends. Keep trying.

There are two rules. First, as you cook, watch it constantly; and secondly always use the right kind of rice. There are three varieties of risotto rice, the most common being Arborio and Carnaroli, and Vialone Nano, which has much smaller grains.

All risottos follow more or less the same principles. You need a wide, heavy-bottomed pan. In this, soften finely chopped shallot in a

generous amount of butter or extra virgin olive oil. At the same time, heat the stock in a separate pan without bringing it to the boil. When all is sizzling, add the rice, stirring it smoothly and making sure every grain is coated. Once it is starting to heat, start to add the hot stock slowly, a little at a time, stirring it in smoothly. As with all recipes, a decent bouillon powder or bought stock will do as long as it is made from the best ingredients (check the label).

If you are flavouring the risotto with something strong, like porcini, vanilla or a potent herb like sage, thyme or oregano, add it at this stage. The rice will start to expand as it gets softer. Risotto shouldn't have too many ingredients but can handle a few layers of flavour. It always benefits from a bit of alcohol: wine, pastis, vermouth and even vodka can add to the delicate flavour balance. Towards the end of cooking you should start to add the ingredients that don't need cooking. Because rice is quite starchy, like pasta, and can go a bit stodgy, mix in some cream and grated Parmesan at the end of cooking, which makes it all the more luxurious.

Sometimes, you may want a risotto that is looser and more like a stew. Some of your first tries might end up like this anyway, but soon you'll get the hang of it and work out just how to create the texture and consistency you want.

Things on Toast

As Nigel Slater has celebrated, toast is a timeless pleasure. And a quick win. Spread with butter it is heavenly. Tapenade, that concoction of olives, olive oil, garlic, lemon juice, black pepper, anchovies, and sun-dried tomatoes was invented to be spread on toasted sourdough. Somehow in that merging of strong tastes and deeply concentrated elements of sunshine and sea, it becomes so much more than the sum of its parts, making the taste-buds bristle with expectation.

Which rather sums up the business of eating things with toast. They are often made of ingredients which on their own are too rich or overpowering but when tempered with a crisp slice, they become alarmingly moreish – their strength filling your palate with flavour. This means that things on toast serve both as snack or supper, as well as something to tease your appetite into excitement at the beginning of a dinner.

But the winning combination doesn't stop at that. With a bit of nerve you can serve up anything on the best toast. A can of baked beans decanted into a pan and warmed with a dash of Worcestershire sauce, fresh black pepper and a very well known brand of mayonnaise makes for the smartest lazy meal ever. Try baby spring vegetables sautéed in butter and cream, served on toast with bacon. Or just mash an avocado on to the toast and drizzle on some olive oil, balsamic vinegar and a sprinkling of salt.

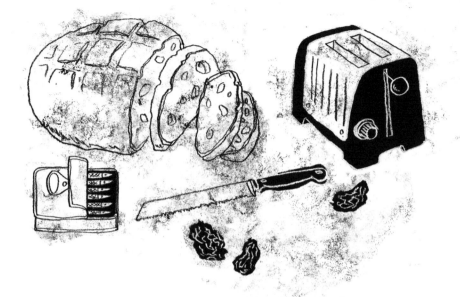

Things like hummus or taramasalata are reliable winners. It's almost impossible to get them wrong and they work for all seasons and appetites. Pâtés made from chicken or duck livers, cold game or fish are also easy for anyone learning to cook.

For the novice cook, these combinations work because the end result doesn't have to look like anything in particular. You can afford to experiment. Even if it goes awry from your original plan, the addition of an extra ingredient or so will transform your pâté into something extraordinary and no-one else will be any the wiser. The trick is to make sure your toast is piping hot and that you serve whatever the melange is on your best plates.

The king of accompaniments for the crispiest melba toast is, of course, *pâté de foie gras*, more often in restaurants a *parfait* made from a combination of ingredients. Now whatever your feelings about the method of producing it (those arguments are well rehearsed elsewhere), here we simply accept that it's an available ingredient. And mouth-watering at that.

Another guilty pleasure on toast, if you are feeling rich but completely lazy and have only the energy to cut a lemon in half and pop a bottle of bubbly, is to screw open a jar of sustainably farmed caviar from Latvia and savour the ultimate eggs on toast, or more traditionally with those tiny pancakes called *blinis*, which are a bit like tiny Scotch drop scones. An alternative, however, to the otherwise unnecessary killing of sturgeon is the Avruga herring roe available in shops and supermarkets. There is plenty of that around because at the moment no-one wants to eat much herring.

Taramasalata is made from cod's roe, so it's bad. Even if you can lay your hands on cod's roe from Icelandic stocks, which trace their provenance down to the shoaling area and means they are not from over-fished stock, then you're lucky. But it's probably unethical for the modern cook to eat the eggs of a rapidly dwindling species of fish. The eggs are, after all, the ocean's future fish stock. In Greece they use carp's roe, so here's hoping that it may become more generally available.

As with most dishes, you should start with something traditional that you know or like. It helps you to improve it if you know what you're expecting.

Tapenade is the easiest to start with. You're aiming for somewhere between a sharp, lemony tang and the richness of olives and sun-dried tomatoes. It's really the simplest thing because you can just keep adding things until you get a combination you like. My favourite is a melange of sun-dried or roasted tomatoes (leave in the oven on a slow heat for hours until all the moisture is gone out of them), anchovies, black olives, flat leaf parsley, lemon juice and grated zest, garlic, paprika and olive oil.

Hummus always wins points with vegetarians, especially with a few winning extras like pounded coriander seeds and cayenne pepper. You blend a tin of chickpeas with an amount of sesame paste, called *tahini*, dependent on your taste. Add finely chopped garlic, lemon juice and olive oil. This is better left overnight to allow the flavours to infuse, otherwise the raw garlic makes it a bit harsh.

Pâtés follow pretty much the same principles. You are blending rich flavours, like chicken livers or smoked salmon, with melted butter, cream, seasonings, sometimes breadcrumbs, herbs and a splash of booze. For chicken or duck livers, gently fry them first but leave them a little pink so that you get that nice colour when you spread the pâté. They really benefit from brandy or sherry at the end of cooking. Mackerel needs more lemon juice than salmon to cut through the oiliness.

Perfect Pasta

Gone are the bad old days when pasta first came on general release outside Italy, served with mounds of ratatouille or mince bolognaise. There are still many British pub restaurants or canteens that don't quite get it and serve pasta treated to the accompaniment of chips. But mostly today we have a somewhat more sophisticated understanding of how it works.

The simplest thing to say about pasta is that because as an ingredient it 'catches' flavours so well, less is more. Whether you are experimenting with home-made pastas or the dried variety, it's no longer necessary to treat it as so much carbohydrate ballast rather than using it as a robust foundation for some interesting combinations. It can easily be swamped by the ingredients you add to it. Just imagine it. Why would Italians have gone to all the trouble of making all those delicate shapes and different lengths of pasta if it was all the same, or if it disappears without trace, drowned in sauce?

It turns out there are more than a thousand different shapes, many created by manufacturers for exciting marketing purposes, others that are traditionally festive or local specialities. When you are buying your pasta, just think about what you are going to cook with it. Different kinds of ingredient will attach to curves, ridges and holes: macaroni for soup, smooth egg linguine and tagliatelli for creamy sauces or seafood, the ridges of penne for catching pesto or a chunky tomato base, and the little bow-ties of fusilli match the delicacy of smoked salmon and capers.

Baked pasta dishes such as cannelloni and lasagne require a lot of meat and sauce to cook the sheets or fill the tubes, so do make sure you have enough for that to happen. These are perfect for using up leftover meats which you can mince, chop finely with herbs and sauce and then add a béchamel sauce to cover the dish. Britain's own take on pasta, macaroni cheese, can also be made in this way.

Stuffed pastas like tortellini, ravioli and agnelotti come from different parts of Italy and are filled with different things. Again because of the delicacy of the fillings, these should not be overwhelmed by too much accompaniment. A little of the greenest young sage or flat leaf parsley cooked in butter will do.

So the basic rule for cooking any pasta is simple. Get the water boiling vigorously in your large pan because if you don't cook it in sufficient water, it will emerge starchy and unpleasant. If you are cooking it fresh for only a few minutes, then it takes much less water. Salting the water is also vital to add some flavour at this point but the oil some recommend isn't really necessary at this stage as it just floats on the surface of the water and disappears once you have drained the pasta. If you are making a sauce or want to loosen the dish up later, keep a little of the cooking liquor. The next stage in some Italian kitchens is to add the grated Parmesan. This sticks to the surface of the pasta first, giving it a strong flavour whatever the sauce. This is excellent when cooking the Venetian classic *bigoli co le sardele salae*, a dish of pasta with salted sardines and onions.

Keep the ingredients interesting and tempting. Think how mouth-watering it is to see a plate of *taglierini al vongole* with some clams peeping out and lemon zest grated over the top. Toasted pine nuts or walnuts bring a welcome crunchiness. Parmesan cheese has become synonymous with pasta but bear in mind that it can have a dominating effect. There is a potential *faux pas* in having cheese with seafood pasta but plenty of traditional Italian dishes call for the combination, so it was clearly just a fashion that stuck. But the point remains, don't overload a pasta dish. Possibly the king of all pasta dishes is the simplest: *pasta con olio y aglio y peperoncito*, simply spaghetti served with chilli, garlic, pepper and olive oil.

A Little Offal

It's easy to dismiss offal. Though it used to be common on plates, in the world of packaged supermarket produce there is something daring and scary about the thought of cooking the 'bits'. Today there are its exponents such as the English chef and writer Fergus Henderson with his 'nose to tail' philosophy. Not a tail, ear, trotter, heart or any innards go unused in his menus; he has a full respect for the whole beast. Nothing is wasted, everything is treasured for its potential, including his signature dish, roasted bone marrow served with parsley salad.

If you are going to cook offal, make sure that smells can't travel from your kitchen to other parts of your home and that you have excellent ventilation. You don't need to have a big offal repertoire but when

kidneys or a nice piece of liver catch your eye in the butcher, you should have a go at cooking them. They are a bargain meal, abounding in all things nutritious, and if you prepare them with love they can taste *haute cuisine*. In fact, delicately prepared and cooked, the taste of lambs' kidneys is almost the same as *foie gras*. After all, they are practically the same thing.

Sometimes kidneys are sold in their own suet, a sort of protective fat, so before cooking, just remove it and any blemish that doesn't look like healthy kidney, then slice them longways. Lightly coat them in flour and season with sea salt and pepper, then drop them into a frying pan of slightly sizzling butter and fry for a few minutes each side. Slosh a large (great-aunt size) glass of Pedro Ximinez sweet sherry into the pan. Traditionally you can use a strong, reduced stock but it isn't always rich enough and the sherry gives the dish a caramelised flavour. Cook the liquid off quickly and in the last moments throw in a handful of chopped tarragon and enough cream to give it a velvety consistency. Serve it mounted on a couple of rounds of toasted brioche (it needs to be something light that will soak up the cream sauce).

Calves' liver, like all offal, gets tough, so it's best to slice it thinly before cooking in butter. Coating it in a little flour can help to cook the outside without browning too much and keep the inside nice and pink. Again you need a strong accompanying flavour to offset liver, so season it well and add herbs and wine or balsamic vinegar.

Oxtail is an off-cut to be relished. You can simply stew it gently with some root vegetables for a few hours until the meat is falling off the bone. But it's very fatty and gelatinous, so if you have the time, let it cool properly, remove the old vegetables and skim off the fat. Then reheat with some fresh cooked vegetables and serve with mashed potatoes.

If you are very confident and patriotic Scot, you might fancy making haggis. You'll need get hold of the lamb's 'lights'. This comprises the heart, lungs and liver. These will have been completely cleaned before leaving the abattoir. Ask for the windpipe to be removed. You'll need two lots of lights for a haggis to serve six people. Add to the shopping list a length of ox intestine, some suet, pinhead oatmeal, onions and spices. Then the fun starts.

In a large pan of salted water, simmer the offal for a couple of hours. While that's happening you'll want to toast up the oatmeal and fry the onions in butter. Then decide what spices you want to use. Allspice is the standard but you could use anything. Mix and roughly mince the cooked meat, oatmeal, onions, suet and your seasonings. Add a little stock for the right consistency.

Now take the intestine and, a bit like mending a stocking, roll it over your hand and arm. Stuff it carefully with your mixture, rolling it back and tying it at both ends, leaving plenty of room for the oats to expand. Cook for three hours in water and serve with the requisite accompaniments and ceremony. If you have got this far, then be justly proud of your self-sufficiency. I suspect you will only do this once.

Sweetbreads is one of those names that belies the truth. They are a combination of various innards taken from young lamb or calves: *thymus* and *pancreas*. Again, preparing them can be quite complicated and not recommended for a kitchen in a bijou urban apartment. They can be soaked overnight and then blanched quickly in boiling water with salt and lemon juice. Compressing the sweetbreads for a few hours between tea towels will make them easier to slice and cook, which is best done by frying or grilling and serving with a sauce or in breadcrumbs.

Stir-Fries

The clarity and focus in the flavour of South-East Asian foods is an antidote to European cooking. They are perhaps closest to the southern Mediterranean countries in the use of spices, chilli and citrus elements to enhance the dishes. Like so many cuisines from other continents, it's hard to replicate these without access to the right ingredients and even the same climate in which to enjoy them. Eating a hot galangal soup for breakfast in Thailand just wouldn't work in Bognor Regis. Nevertheless, there's a lot to learn from this immediate, fresh style of cooking, where you can bring whole dishes together in a matter of minutes.

Much of what makes oriental food stand out is the way it is prepared and the freshness of the ingredients used. When you are making a stir-fry, you need to have all the vegetables cut and ready before you start cooking. It's a useful example of how you prepare ingredients differently to ensure the outcome you want. In a wok, the metal is thin and the heat is uniformly very hot, which is why you must keep stirring and turning the contents. Use a metal spoon so that it slips easily round the ingredients, rather than a wooden spoon which will crush the edges of the vegetables and make the end result mushy. If you are using tougher vegetables you need to cut them to the size and shape you'd like to eat, bearing in mind they'll take longer to cook. Typically most things need to be thin and shredded and you add whatever will take longest to cook first. Don't use ingredients that exude lots of water, so if you are using mushrooms, choose the smaller oriental varieties and add them right at the end; the same with courgettes. And get your flavouring ingredients, like chilli, ginger, garlic and lime, in the wok early so that they infuse the whole dish.

So, put some sesame oil in your hot wok and, without letting it smoke, start immediately adding first carrots and baby aubergines, then peppers, then add some mangetout or pak choi, ending with your spring onions, which want to be green and slightly crunchy. Remember this kind of cooking is all about colour and texture so you don't want to end up with something resembling ratatouille. Err on the side of caution as everything will keep cooking a bit when it's in the wok. If you are eating it with noodles, make sure they are nice and dry before adding them to the wok at the end. You can, in fact, finish the noodles off by stir-frying them separately in the wok, so they get a bit crispy.

You need to judge when whatever meat or fish you are using should go into the dish. Again you don't want too much moisture, so if it's been sitting in a marinade, make sure it has dried out a bit. Keep whatever it is to thin strips that won't overwhelm the end result. At the end of cooking, you might want to add a bit of soy sauce for flavour, while a handful of freshly chopped coriander works wonders for the eye, particularly if things have gone a bit limp.

Stir-frying is an engaging way to deliver vegetables to the table with any dish. Because so much of the freshness remains in them, you can bring some powerful flavours to the meal, rather than the vegetables always coming in a poor second. You can also use a wok to shallow-fry your chicken or fish goujons, and if you learn to make a bit of batter, tempura is joyfully done this way.

Vegetable Matters

Vegetables get a raw deal and are all too often treated as second best. Though we talk about them a great deal elsewhere in this book, this needs to be emphasised. It's surprising that despite the encouraging improvements in cooking generally, vegetables still so often appear waterlogged and old-school, like an amateur church choir. When, compared to meat and fish, growing vegetables is fairly sustainable, it's a travesty that dreary carrots, cauliflower and the ubiquitous broccoli, flaccid mushrooms and greenish beans remain the mainstay of so many tables. And more to the point, that they are cooked on the side with no attention to the enticement of our taste-buds, even in the best restaurants. They need to be cooked with love and care, be dressed in the finest ways and made to feel special. Then you will luxuriate in every bite and wonder why you eat meat at all.

When there isn't much left in the provisions box except a very large bag of carrots, all hope is not lost. The addition of some toasted walnuts, crumbled feta cheese and chopped mint creates a feast. Even the most common vegetables can be brought to new life with some imagination. We get stuck cooking the usual suspects in the same ways, ignoring the fact that some are better cold or raw in salads or that they love having their flavours coaxed out in different ways,

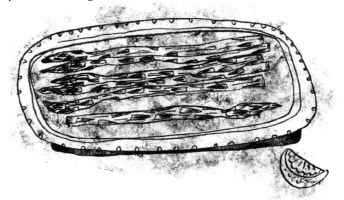

with herbs, spices, lemons and seasonings. Even though I am a fan of cauliflower cheese, in Italy I was served cold florets as a starter, sprinkled with rich green olive oil, oregano, sea salt, black pepper and Parmesan. Unimaginable perfection.

For years, the poor vegetarian has been relegated to meatless lasagne and risotto, never allowed to move beyond goat cheese tartlets. When it comes to veggies, exercise aplomb and a pioneering spirit in your culinary matchmaking. Go for things you don't recognise or haven't had before. There is always a literal cornucopia of new and interesting contenders. Things like celeriac roasted with cumin, or golden beetroots made into a lemon-creamy soup. Be inventive and free with what you find in your favourite shops. It doesn't have to be only the exotic. Among the usual suspects, green beans are wonderful with shallots, tarragon and tomatoes, cabbage a delicacy cooked in sesame oil and caraway seeds, and in winter try a few anchovies mashed into Brussels sprouts. Each brings something exclusive to the party and sometimes they actually steal the show. A perfectly slow-baked potato, with spinach and a creamy, wine sauce, a plate of buttered baby broad beans, or roasted squash with thyme are as good a fine dining experience as you can have anywhere.

With the vast selection of vegetables from all over the world easily available, we should be imaginative in our choices. It will help you as a cook to sometimes forgo anything but vegetables and try to do interesting things with them.

For me the finest of all vegetables, notwithstanding its malodorous emetic properties, is asparagus. Both the summery green English shoots and the stout white stems you find in jars. It's apparently aphrodisiac, so you have a chance of getting more than a good dinner and it's utterly simple to prepare, asparagus is a Barbie doll of a vegetable. You can dress it up with anything from butter, parmesan, eggs and truffles and it still retains its elegant appearance. To cook, it's equally simple. You can grill, steam, stir-fry, pop it in the microwave or even slice it raw into salads. But beware, like all girly dates, overdo it and she'll go cold on you. Observe restraint and you'll be satisfied. For the purist there are only two months in the British calendar from April to June, when asparagus is harvested, so it's a short fling. Naturally, they are flying in her foreign cousins all year round these days.

Getting Saucy

There was a time in British cooking when every dish was smothered in a sauce of some shape or variety. There was a mistaken belief that this was the 'French' way. Though the flair and assiduity of French cooking has mastered the art of creating exceptional and mouth-watering sauces, they need to be used judiciously and sparingly. Too often restaurants that aspire to the higher reaches of fine dining kill their dishes dead with over-use of foams and emulsions, not allowing the real stars of the plate to sparkle.

This book is about giving you the understanding of the essential information about dishes and it's up to you to decide when you add something or the way you cook it. But as always, it's useful to be armed with a few of the basics under your belt. And there are probably four or five sauces that are useful to be able to whisk up. What they almost all share is that they require both constant stirring and the very gradual introduction of the liquid.

Béchamel is white sauce. It's a versatile standard of cookery and can be adapted and flavoured in many different ways. You start by creating a sort of thickening agent called the roux, to which you add liquid and seasonings as it gradually becomes a sauce. To make a roux, simply melt butter in a pan until it starts to clarify, which means the butter is sizzling and starts to run clear (careful not to let it go brown and if it does, start again). Depending on how much sauce you want, add a spoonful or two of plain white flour and stir it steadily to a thick, smooth, buttery paste. Season at this point with some finely ground pepper and salt. Next you add milk (or cream), keeping the whole reaction moving over a low heat, with a spoon or small whisk, so the sauce doesn't go lumpy. Gradually add more milk until you get the consistency and quantity you want. To begin with you may not get the quantities exactly right; if this happens all you do is make a little more quite liquid roux and add it in to the sauce.

If you are making a moussaka, you'll add some ground mace or nutmeg to the béchamel when seasoning. But for cauliflower cheese or parsley sauce, add your extra ingredient once the sauce is well on its way.

Some roast meats don't produce a lot of liquid, so you can make a gravy by adding a little roux to the roasting pan at the end of cooking and loosen with wine or water as it thickens.

The next family of sauces is made using a reaction of acid on egg yolks, followed by the introduction of oil or butter. These are mayonnaise and hollandaise. Almost the only difference is that the latter is hot. There is no doubt that mayonnaise takes a lot of practice but whatever the initial outcome, it's always going to be finer than a shop-bought variety and is usually always salvageable if it does go wrong.

For mayonnaise, begin with a couple of egg yolks in the bottom of a bowl. I prefer to use a big bowl with high sides so it doesn't splatter everywhere. Mix in a little mustard (powder or paste), healthy splashes of white wine vinegar or tarragon vinegar, salt and pepper and, if you like, a little squeeze of lemon. Stir this gently then, using an electric whisk on a low speed, very slowly drizzle oil into the mixture until it starts to thicken and slowly get stiffer. Olive oil is heavier than others, like grapeseed, so it can be a good idea to use a mixture of oils to keep the final result quite light and green. It's a substance called lecithin in the egg yolk that stabilises the mixture in this way, so if you find your mayonnaise separating, just start again with your whisk. Adding a spoon of boiling water will stabilise the mixture.

Hollandaise is pretty much the same but, since it is a hot sauce, you have to be careful not to let the egg yolks get hot otherwise they end up cooking. It can be made in different ways, depending on whether you have machinery or prefer to go the double-boiler route. Here you are slowly mixing melted butter into the egg yolk (you might use double the quantity for a super-luxury sauce), vinegar, lemon juice and seasonings. This can be done as you pour the melted butter slowly into a liquidiser, or equally you can stir the butter bit by bit into a bowl to melt into the other ingredients as the sauce thickens.

From mayonnaise, you can make a variety of other sauces. *Rouille*, which is used to put on the croûtons in *bouillabaisse*, requires the addition of garlic, saffron and cayenne pepper. To make a tartare sauce from mayonnaise, add some capers, finely chopped *cornichons* and chives. *Aioli* is a staple Spanish garlic mayonnaise. The garlic is best pounded to a paste using your pestle and mortar and if you can find wild garlic leaves, chop them finely into the sauce. This is best left overnight for the garlic to infuse fully and lose its backbite.

The secret of a strong tomato sauce is to use good-quality Italian tinned tomatoes. But before decanting them into the pan, you squeeze all of the watery tomato liquid out of the tin so you are only left with the flesh. This means about four tins for quite a small amount of sauce. Cut a very generous amount of garlic into large slices. Add to extra virgin oil in your pan with some green peppercorns, freshly cracked black pepper and salt. When the garlic is about to go brown, empty the prepared tomatoes into the pan. Have the lid handy as it will spit vigorously. Now just leave it to reduce slowly, for a minimum of an hour (the more tins, the longer it will take). If the sauce is for meatballs or something meaty, you may want to add red wine and let that reduce. If it's for a fishy pasta use white wine.

There are plenty of other sauces you might want to get fresh with but if you can master these and play around with their ingredients you will have a solid repertoire with which to show off your dishes to any audience.

The Cheese Board

Cheese is like wine, so much is it an expression of the combination of where it comes from, the natural and human processes it undergoes, the maturation and ultimately the circumstances under which it is relished by the human palate. The normal habit was for

cheese to be eaten more or less immediately in the area where it was made. But early in the twentieth century in France, smart suppliers began buying the artisanal products from across France and selling them in their shops. Paris cheesemongers became the hallmark of excellence based on their expertise for ageing cheese in the micro-climate of their cellars under the boulevards. This involved washing the rinds in brine or alcohol and tending the cheeses every day. Today there are many fine examples of this maturing skill in Britain.

We've all walked into a specialist cheese shop and suffered rising panic. With no real understanding of how different cheeses taste and why, it's easy to feel at sea. But a good cheesemonger will put you at your ease and offer a taste of anything before you buy. This can be a problem for some people who think they do know about cheese and make some of the obvious mistakes, the most common of which is to buy too much. We assume we should haul home great chunks of the stuff. Instead you should be looking for three or four contrasting varieties, enough to enjoy on one occasion. It is the cheesemonger's skill to mature and sell the cheese just at the right time. The longer you keep it at home, the more quickly it will suffer under fluctuating temperatures.

So what about eating cheese? Being British and obsessed by class, as with wine, we've developed some silly snobbishness about it. First up, you can eat it when and how you want. There is no particular rule about before or after pudding – it rather depends on what you like. Clearly after savoury dishes, it can help your digestion to have something sweet. But for lots of people, their palate can't go back and forth like that. In France it differs from country to region and family to town.

Nor does it matter how you cut cheese, though generally you'd slice a soft cheese from outside in so that you get a full cut. It's worth having a cheese knife that allows you to peel slivers of hard cheese because you taste the flavours more intensely. But sometimes a cheese is perfect for an aperitif or you might just eat a cheese from Burgundy, like *Epoisse*, baked with some white wine and eaten with bread.

And be adventurous with your accompanying drink. Bordeaux is generally far too heavy for and masks the delicacy of everything but blue cheese. You might want to try a white Burgundy or even Champagne to wash it down. Even better, find a wine produced in the same *terroir* and you'll be approaching something near cheese heaven.

Uncomplicated Puddings

Puddings, desert, afters or sweets are a challenge. Often this is because they arrive on the table at the end of the meal, which means that while your fellow diners have been making merry, scoffing away from the dishes on offer and quaffing wine, you've still had to think about the last thing being cooked. Which is why it makes sense to have a cold pudding.

There is such an expertise in putting together puddings. You only have to look into the window of the patisserie to see the creative endeavour that goes into crafting some of these extraordinary confections. It takes years to train to be able to perform with such ability. Twirls of caramelised banana pavlova, frangipane pear tart or Muscat soufflé take a bit more than attitude and energy. You can only start on those when you've acquired patience and an eye for detail.

However, if you want to cook without recipes or adapt the ones you like, then you need to build your skills without giving yourself too big a challenge. And what could be simpler to start with than rice pudding? Firm, creamy, with a lemony zest and crisp skin. You bring the milk to the bubble with thin strips of lemon zest, a few spoons of caster sugar to taste and a few drops of vanilla essence. Add the washed pudding rice (two handfuls for half a litre of milk or cream) and simmer for five minutes. Then pour the whole lot into a buttered dish with some tiny knobs of butter and scrapings of nutmeg. Cover and cook in a moderate oven until creamy, then grill if you love the skin. Stodgy, warm, filling and sweet.

Another show-stopper of English dining is summer pudding, recalling those days when the smell of crushed grass and the hum of darting insects are the boon companions of a tinkling glass of chilled wine and a plate of fine food. These are the dream days of life, when the cold silk of river waters and the gentle warmth of the sun on our skin renders back to us all, our childhood selves.

Ideally made with a stale white loaf, you can cheat by leaving slices of cheap white bread out for a few hours. This is the quintessence of summer fruit puddings – gooseberries, red and blackcurrants and raspberries – inside a bread dome, oozing with sugary, tart juices. And it's simply done. Put the berries in a pan and add sugar – about eighty:twenty or to your liking. Let the juices run and, if necessary, add a little juice (or even water) to help them along. Let them bubble joyfully for a while but don't let the fruits disintegrate. While this is going on, you want to cut the crust-less slices of bread to line a large bowl that will hold the pudding, saving a couple of pieces for the top. Pour the juices from the pan over the bread first, making sure it's fully soaked, then spoon in the fruit, finally adding more slices and juice to cover. Then squeeze a small plate over the whole and weigh it down with whatever you can find. Leave it overnight. Just before you serve it with rich, yellow double cream, turn it out of the basin on to a lovely dish.

Buying an ice-cream machine will serve you well and allow you to freshly churn amazing concoctions of ingredients that will make your guests very greedy. For my book, a little plate of ice-cream with some *amarettini* biscuits, *speculos* or *langues de chat* is the perfect pudding. You can use everything from marmalade and cottage cheese to lemon curd, comb honey, green chartreuse and stewed plums. Add cream to your mixture, make sure the whole will be sweet enough and switch on the machine. You can add crunchy bits like puff candy or meringue to give it some texture.

If you grew up in the 1970s you can have fun recreating the knickerbocker glory with mixed fruits topped by whipped cream and strawberry and chocolate ice-cream, with flaked almonds and any kind of sugary shaken frippery.

Eton mess was born on the cricket fields of that school, so is another quintessentially British dish combining strawberries, cream and meringue. But it's a style of pudding that should suit most creative cooks, allowing you to bring together any combination of ingredients. You can make a Christmas pudding mess, which makes the experience of eating the heavy suet mincemeat after that huge festive meal, a little more manageable.

A fruit crumble is relatively easy without having to stray too far into the world of baking. All you have to do is to sprinkle the sweet crumbly mixture over your fruit, which might be a bit stewed, and let it crisp up in the oven. Rub flour and sugar together with plenty of butter and drip a little cold water over it so you get it slightly lumpy. There is a quince version (they need to be peeled and simmered in water for at least an hour), where you can make the crumble into a paste and dribble it over the juicy gaps in between the orangey stewed fruit. When it cooks, this bakes in the liquid and it makes for an interesting variation of the traditional version. You can, of course, add spices such as cinnamon and ginger to the crumble or directly into the fruit.

I suppose that a compendium of easy puddings wouldn't be complete without something chocolatey. Chocolate pots are probably the most fun and popular, particularly as making them involves a fair amount of finger licking. You heat up some double cream and melt chocolate into it so that it's a smooth, thick sauce before whisking a couple of egg yolks and a knob or two of butter into the mix. If you want it to be boozy, now's the time to add some Cointreau or brandy. Decant this sumptuous sweetness into whatever you plan to serve it in.

Cooking Breakfast

This uniquely British institution has stood the test of time and travelled successfully around the world. And not only are its elements versatile and easy to learn, they present the cook with some superb opportunities to impress. From the romantic moment of breakfast in bed with your lover to rediscovering one's faculties after a one-night stand, this national treasure is worth mastering.

Above all, cooked breakfast requires quantity and quality. Too often,

even good cooks disregard these virtues. There is nothing less appetising than pusillanimous eggs, unfathomably meatless sausages, uncooked, watery tomatoes and mushrooms as soggy as a Scotsman's bonnet. Too often people think you can just shove the elements together without thought for every right and proper element of this most noble repast.

A fried breakfast needs to pack a punch sufficient to see off bilious reflux and rising nausea. It should be a flavoursome, enriching ballast; a mix of soul food and blood-strengthening fuel. Enough to see you through the newspapers and a black and white movie, then induce afternoon slumber. Buying the best meat possible is therefore essential and these days there is no shortage of great butchers making big claims on the sausage front. The same goes for bacon. It's said that cooking bacon is the most universally tempting smell in Western cuisine, even for vegetarians and religious zealots. Serving it up like a flabby napkin of leather with a rind of snot doesn't quite reach that accolade. You want thick slices with lots of strong fat. This is vital in a fry-up. At the end you want these two sizzling in a slew of extra virgin oil and garlic, with tomatoes reduced to messy red, slightly burned sludge, infusing the whole in a feast of colour. Likewise you need to fry the buggery out of mushrooms so that there is no water slopping around. Suddenly they will add an earthy, fungus tinge.

So for breakfast worth a hero's return, here goes. Take your best (cooking should always be like going on a date), deepest and widest pan and pour in a small puddle of the finest olive oil you can find. Add a large knob of butter for nutty good measure. Slice in a clove of garlic, chopped sage, salt and fresh broken peppercorns. Now add your top-end sausages and bacon. When it's all browning, add halved baby plum tomatoes – or just some variety with a chance of flavour. Press them down with the back of a spoon so that the juices escape into the oil. While they sizzle, soak slices of bread in the rusty, buttery oil and allow to brown on both sides. Add the mushrooms now, if you want. Get all the water out of them – they should be like toffee. Ensure the sausages and fat of the bacon are well done; overcook them if necessary. When you are ready to serve it all, make some space in the pan and drop in your eggs – the oil needs to be hot enough for the whites to 'seize' on the spot and not spread out everywhere. At this point, you could also cast some wafers of truffle or chopped porcini to marshal that big, nosey flavour to your eggs. If you like them sunny-side down, flip the eggs over. Otherwise pop them on to the crisp bread nestling in the tomatoey goo and mushrooms. Rank your meats alongside and you'll feel as proud as a general trooping the colour.

There are many other versions of breakfast, particularly for vegetarians. These can be equally noble dishes. Eggs Florentine is one, in which you poach the eggs and serve them on spinach wilted in butter, lemon juice and pepper and coat the top with luxuriously buttery hollandaise. Lightly whisked eggs, poured into a pan with spring onions softening in butter and served with fresh sorrel will revive an ailing parent. And over-easy scrambled eggs cooked with a little cream and eaten with lightly toasted wholemeal bread is said to be one of the most nutritious and healthy meals you can eat. The addition of fish, such as smoked salmon or haddock, will raise the whole game and bring up the protein level. But for the lighter appetite, the young or the sick, nothing is required but the whitest bread to be toasted, crusts off, sliced into soldiers and dipped after four minutes into the yellowest egg yolk you can find.

Breakfast wouldn't be complete without the accompaniment of marmalade for your toast. At some mysterious moment in early January, the Seville oranges will appear in a wooden box on the street outside your local grocer. Time for marmalade again. Twelve oranges makes enough for the year, though your guests may sometimes get a little greedy. If you have an electric juicer, squeeze out the juice, pith and pips, otherwise do it by hand. The correct thing to do is to tie this 'pomace' into a muslin cloth and put it in a very large pan – you need to allow plenty of bubbling room. But you can use a plastic sieve that sits just submerged at the top of the waterline. The idea is to get the natural pectin out, so, as always, do whatever works best for you. Next, boil the orange halves lightly in water for a couple of hours until they are soft. Slice them to whatever thickness you like. Remove the muslin and add the sugar. Dark muscovado gives it a really strong, grown-up taste but you need to add some granulated to get the right syrupy consistency later.

For every two kilos of oranges you need to start with more or less five litres of water (which evaporates by a third during the simmering) and then double the amount of sugar as oranges. Get this sugary, dark orange mixture bubbling like a witch's cauldron, which takes around half an hour. Keep stirring it and be very careful that the sugar doesn't 'catch' the pan and burn on the bottom. When it looks thick and can catch on a cold spoon without dripping off, take it off the heat and decant into jars.

You'll need fantastic bread upon which to eat your deep, rich spread, so why not make your own? You don't need to be an expert baker and even the least bold cook can achieve a pretty good loaf with patience and persistence, as witnessed by the massive rise in the popularity of the pleasure of baking. As with everything else, only use the best ingredients you can lay your hands on. Fresh yeast is available from almost any supermarket and most bakers will sell you a little. Otherwise strong, unrefined white flour, really good salt and a bit of warm water are all you need. You should check your favourite baking writers for the measurements, as they will vary depending on the kind of bread you prefer. But the secret is in the kneading. Find an open space; a table top or marble work surface is best. When you have your mixture at the right consistency, you need to start pulling and stretching it and folding it over itself. A bit of slapping about and pounding with your fists can help too. But it's getting air into the mix that's essential. And doing it for long enough that you get the dough to rise during 'proving', where you leave it alone in a warm place to let the yeast do its thing. This needs a couple of hours, so you need to have thought ahead or at least have one stored in the freezer to pull out for such occasions.

It's simply unacceptable not to carry off a Bloody Mary with the finest cooked breakfast. This drink is the perfect antidote to the morning after. It ought to be a shock to the system, something to surprise the palate and shake off surfeit – like getting an unexpected dressing down from an ageing maiden aunt. All the chill sharpness and pique of horseradish, Tabasco, vodka and lemon, tempered by the potpourri of Worcestershire sauce and celery salt and topped with the sombre, self-assured experience of sherry and rich tomato. A Lady Bracknell of drinks. And if it turns out like a date with a librarian – all limp, sour smirks and over-washed winceyette knickers – you can just butch it up with as many more of the above ingredients as necessary. You'll soon concoct something that will blow off any residue of past sins.

A Survival Guide
to Shopping

Shopping for food, like everything else, has become a war of attrition. It usually means rushing headlong to the nearest supermarket. And let's face it, they are unremittingly brash and unrewarding places. We load up trolleys in a state somewhere between hysteria and panic, depending whether we are accompanied by a young child or a partner who spends the entire experience immersed in a taxing mental negotiation between the benefits of varying brands of cholesterol-lowering yoghurt drink.

Alternatively, we'll write up a detailed list from a recipe book and double our pain wandering aimlessly up aisles looking for things we never knew existed before and will most likely never use again. Intimidated by price and choice – usually both – we're just too tired or busy to care. Then we make a quick exit, counting some blessings, and arrive home in a muck sweat with a two-metre long receipt. From the results of which we have to piece it all together.

That is for most of us. There are, of course, some fortunate enough to simply slip into the food hall of some fabulous department store to stock up on life's little necessaries. And these are a unique shopping experience, albeit knee-shakingly expensive. More akin to sliding on a very sheer denier stocking before a cocktail party or being transported to sleep in a summer garden with the scent of honeysuckle and the sound of a Chopin prelude. But because the producers of such delights are only marketing to a very small demographic, very occasionally it's just what you're looking for.

This may sound idyllic, but with the busy lives we lead, who has time for all that shunting around fancy shops and looking for the perfect ingredients? That's why it's so important to stock the quality staples in your kitchen so that all it takes is the presumptuous entrance of some new ingredient to inspire a nourishing and original dish.

There is of course a middle way. But it requires a leap of faith. You need to have sufficient self-belief to buy instinctively whatever fascinates you. And not to worry about what you will do with it until you get home.

This kind of shopping can take in as many of your favourite emporia as you want. And as it can segue with fashion therapy, drinks and eating, a whole day spent picking up nice produce is fun. It starts with the fishmonger and butcher, who are loud and brash and full of themselves. Their calloused hands deftly handle some of the best produce you can find: wild salmon from Sutherland, aged beef from France, octopus from Galicia and oysters from heaven.

You need to find somewhere to buy the best artisanale French cheeses available, freshly ferried from France, so that you are spoiled with something unique every time you visit.

This may sound like the nearest thing you can have to the Prahan Market in Melbourne or the early morning fish stall on the Riviera, but if they are off-limits, you need to find your favourite place to buy the best ingredients. Even if it means clubbing together with some local friends and getting up at dawn to visit your local wholesale fish or meat market, it will be a revelation.

And the two most important factors in all of this are, firstly that you make friends with the people selling you food. They will love you for talking to them. And secondly, ask questions about everything you are buying; they will respect your thirst for knowledge and, even more, they will enjoy telling you all they know. If they don't, you will always find some that do. More than ever, food is a specialist market. People are committing to develop artisan products with care and attention to detail not seen in recent years. If you're going to enjoy them and proselytise about it, you need to know what you're on about. Plus, it will impress your friends.

But when the road ahead looks tough going, we are rightly asking some questions about the way we spend our money. The years of plenty and fat-fleshed kine were well favoured for food shops and restaurants. Less definitely became more, not only where jet fuel, fertilisers and insecticides were concerned.

With the promise of individually harvested, locally sourced, hand-raised, line-caught produce, we've been happy to lash out for any hint of organic produce. Good ingredients have definitely gone gourmet in recent years. Honest provender like decent bread, English apples or a nice old cockerel for the pot have now become rare standards of excellence. But the negative side of this is that somewhat shamefully and in the face of nations almost dying from their processed, fast-food diets, despite the noble attempts to radicalise the food industry, these delicacies remain the preserve of those of us with cash.

But what of free-range, organic, fair-trade, slow-food, food-miles and the other movements that impact on food supply and demand? Well you need to make up your own mind in terms of what you are prepared to buy and, notwithstanding the obvious ethical issues of animal welfare and our depleting oceans, much of it has to be about personal conscience. For vast numbers of people in Africa, the fact that we eat the vegetables they grow sustains their economies, but the fuel we use to fly it around the skies may be impacting on climate change.

We can safely say that free-range is always good. But don't be fooled by the description as legislation seems to have widened the definition as the years go on. The same goes for organic, which is always to be supported but often less important when it comes to animal husbandry. Clearly we don't like our meat to be pumped full of hormones but I'd rather have a clear sense of the life of the beast in the field than worry about a few well-tested drugs to prevent disease.

If you have the money, it is always worth paying a small premium for really good, fresh food and there are many shops and online services where you can find it. But there are equally as many opportunists in the organic revolution. The term itself spells no love of food *per se*. You need to shop smart and spot which sellers are jumping on the bandwagon and who is really throwing themselves into supplying the best foods. A few judiciously placed questions should flush out the charlatans.

Still, for those who are unable to afford this kind of eating, or who have no idea how to begin, it's still a tough world of processed evils out there. And confronted with a chicken that costs the same as a whole weekly shop from a frozen food outlet, what would you do? Supermarkets do watch people's buying habits so by being responsible about what foods we buy will eventually make a difference to what they stock. The increased use of free-range eggs and associated products is a good example of that.

Having said that, it's fine to shop in lots of supermarkets for different products where you know you can get a good deal or a better range. It pays to shop around. Even the supermarkets with the biggest discounts have something worth buying. In the end, it's your creativity that counts. You can start with the humblest ingredients to make a meal worth shouting about. Having little money doesn't prevent you doing that. As long as you put love into what you cook, people will love to eat it. So shopping just requires a sharp eye for quality and a passion for discovery.

Cooks and their Books

Throughout this book, I've made it clear how important it is for the cook to become an aficionado of food writing. Just like painters, actors or any other artists, you will find inspiration from books written by the experts in your field. They will be good friends when the darker days of despair or sullen lack of ideas descends. Like all relationships, you need variety and stimulation from which to depart into your own creative world. People might even say to you that they recognise a recipe from a certain writer. Of course. Few ideas are ever completely original and recipes we think we've invented have often been lurking in the darker pools of our memories or impressed themselves on us from articles or TV programmes. Don't worry – claim it as your own. Cooking is like poetry, a combination of ingredients, ideas and concepts in no particular order. If your creativity is influenced by what you've read, eaten or seen cooked, then it's a good thing, something to be applauded. It means you've become a confident, creative, and above all, attentive cook. There can be no patenting of the preparation and cooking of food. If you are not working in a fast food restaurant or bakehouse, the same dish will never turn out in exactly the same way twice.

You'll want a selection of books across the ages on your shelves, from the illuminating ancients to the quirky specialists, the old faves to the young arrivistes. At different moments you'll prefer books with a narrative which you'd be contented reading in bed, on a plane or on the loo. So modern writers like Tessa Kiros, Ana del Conte, Mary Contini, Simon Hopkinson and even Britain's national culinary writing treasure Nigel Slater, all make for an entrancing storytelling as well as imparting their knowledge with enormous affection.

There is an exact parallel between writing and cooking. Finding a 'voice' as a writer takes time, a voice that people become familiar with and trust. The kind of voice you might want to learn from or be amused by. And writing about food, there is a particular challenge against which only a few outstanding personalities succeed. You will each have your own preferred food writers, some who put more emphasis on the specifics of recipes and others who will open the doors of detail in the history, traditions and background of the dishes they describe.

The best writers put food first. They disappear behind the ingredients and dishes they describe, making them the heroes of the hour. They entice and delight us with the possibilities of cooking and they foreground the creative potential of their readers, never painting themselves as gurus, always excitedly sharing their wisdom as if it was nothing more than happenstance.

Elizabeth David had a gift for writing. And it is precisely because she delighted in language and food that she manages, at her best, to conjure the actual pleasure she experiences. A hard act to follow for any food writer. Her books were beautifully produced with sensitive illustrations by the painter John Minton. Every kitchen should really hold a number of well-thumbed copies to which to turn for entertainment and inspiration. For a whole generation of home cooks, *French Provincial Cooking* (Penguin) knows no rival. It has been reprinted many times and has now even been published anew with the addition of photographs.

For those of you who want to delve deep into the traditions of French cuisine, the great master Escoffier won't actually give you much more than a rather gruffly gallic and comprehensive set of instructions. But Julia Child's collaborative *Mastering the Art of French Cooking* (Particular Books) is a gallop through the great dishes of the nation. Though written particularly for an American culinary sensibility, her exuberance and sense of melodrama about food is irresistible.

Richard Olney was an American painter and writer living in France in 1960s who, like Child, became fascinated with the national virtuosity in cooking and gained a profound knowledge of food and wine. He wrote about it in his newspaper column and then published it in *The French Menu Cookbook* (Collins), in which he presents outstanding seasonal menus with wine pairings. Olney is passionate and fun, combining a delight in detail with a verve for the whole atmosphere and occasion of a summer lunch in Provence. Who could resist?

Though there have been many recipe books produced in Britain over recent decades, it was really Rose Gray and Ruth Rogers who revived the whole genre with new ideas and stylish photography back in the 1980s with their sharp, smart appraisal of regional Italian dishes in the *River Café Cookbook* series (Ebury Press). From them we learned about simple flavour combinations, dramatic possibilities with previously unrewarding ingredients without lavish sauces or complicated cooking procedures. What they taught above all was disarmingly simple technique, which was adopted as the 'throw it in' school of cooking, later snapped up and run with by their Essex child-prodigy Jamie Oliver.

Nigella Lawson and Delia Smith seem to be at opposite ends of the spectrum when it comes to cooking, one appealing to affluent yummy mummies with Sunday supper parties and the other more homely and comforting. But we should never forget that Delia was a tasty TV celebrity cook long before her younger, sexier challenger. And it would be a mistake to underestimate either. If you read no other writers, you'd learn to cook, albeit in different ways, from either. They both have an honesty and authenticity about them. And if they've had to learn to cook through the unrewarding years of motherhood and feeding reluctant children, all credit to them. But for me Nigella takes the biscuit. Notwithstanding the legendary finger-licking, she seems to speak to us with a nonchalant intimacy, coaxing you into cooking without any judgement or sense of superiority. With the merest flick of her hair, you are drawn into the food, the taste and the secrets that lie within. She makes food the star.

Cookery books should be about helping people to aspire to greater things; to learn that it's possible to achieve amazing cooking without knowing anything about *haute cuisine*. It's why Jamie Oliver's early books were such a huge success. With that inimitable, lippy enthusiasm, he reduces some of the snobbish inanities of foaming velouté reductions to 'food loverly food'. Like all good cooks, his books help the learner discover what's already there.

Loving both food and books, your favourites should both delight and inform. There will always be those that capture the essence of what it is to love food. For me, no-one has done that with quite the modest enthusiasm of Nigel Slater. You see, unlike the celebrity chefs, for Slater the *dramatis personae* are those ingredients he loves, touches and tastes. He has an almost slavish and child-like adoration for food and cooking, like a parent talking fondly, if endlessly, about his offspring. And there is something of that doting that slips into his use of language, which he uses as deftly as his kitchen implements and wide knowledge. One of the first images he used that stuck with me describes the 'almost virginal quality to chicory as it lies in its box of deep-blue waxed paper'. If you haven't read *Toast*, his childhood memoir, don't lose a second more before you buy it; enchanting, intense, vivid and sexy.

In the last couple of years, Nigel brought us two volumes of another, highly personal memoir of food. *Tender I* and *II* tell the stories of Slater's love affair with his garden in Islington and the many seedlings he has raised in his box-hedged vegetable patches and fruit garden. They are magnificent volumes, with pictures of his Eden, its produce and many of the recipes he has created from them. His premise is that having done such damage to our environment, meat and fish are increasingly becoming the side dishes. With the variety and quality of vegetables, herbs and fruits available, we can become more imaginative and creative than ever. He brings the side dish to the centre of the table, writing of the smells, sounds and pictures in his kitchen and garden with a greedy eye for detail.

There are so many other books to read, it would be impossible to note them all here. Indeed I'm hoping this book too will become a familiar title on the shelves of many kitchens. But more interesting than any of these is how you develop your own atmosphere, style and love for cooking and eating, how your kitchen comes to reflect the creative genius inside you. Keep your culinary friends close enough to reach out to but always have the independence to step out and up. On your own.

The lesson there then is to keep buying new writers before their marketing machines have them churning out endless re-runs of what they've said before. Catch them at their most original. This book will be out of date by the time a whole new generation of writers will have developed their own style and enthusiasms.

And for that reason, the internet today is a powerful tool for many writers, particularly those who don't want to go through the whole rigmarole of publishing. It's a great training ground for people to develop their writing technique and focus on specific passions in cooking. There is a difference between writing and blogging, between those who try to tell the whole story rather than simply recount their foodie experiences or recipe successes. But the internet is fresh and always new. People are talking about what arrived on their plate today or what happened to a particular ingredient this evening. So look out for your favourites and let them entertain and inform you.

They will bring a freshness and immediacy through the web and social media that your shelves of books might miss.

You should try to use this book as if you were shopping. Of course we hope it will be a help to you, if you want to understand a particular idea or ingredient. But you should also feel that by skimming through it and casting your eye across its pages, that you will light up your curiousity. Read it any way you choose. Chance upon the next dish or style of cooking you want to try out. Be bold, search the corners of your mind and have the courage to cook what you want. And in the manner of the great Julia Child, at the top of your voice shriek 'Bon Appetit'!

Index

A
almonds 55
anchovies 49–50, 117, 133
artichokes 74–75
aubergines 76

B
balsamic vinegar 61
battery farming 92–93
beans 46, 72
béchamel sauce 160
beef 132
bloody Mary 172–173
boiling pans 12–13
books 179–185
bowls 21–22
brassicas 73
bread 172
breakfast 168–173
breakfast, fried 169–170
buckwheat 52, 53
bulgar wheat 52, 53

C
Caesar salad 115
canned vegetables 47
capsicum 75
caraway seeds 56
cardamom seeds 56
carrots, cooking 70
casserole 15, 134, 135
capers 48
carbohydrates 51–52
cashew nuts 55
celeriac, cooking 70
cheese 116, 162–164
chestnut puree 56
chestnuts 56
chicken 92–93, 128
chickpeas 47
chicory 78–79
Child, Julia 181
chocolate pot 168
chopping boards 19–20
clams 124
cleaning 23–24

cockles 124

coffee beans 26

condiments 56–62

cookery books 179–185

cooking oil 30–31

courgettes 77, 109

couscous 53–54

crab 122

croutons 112

crumble 168

crustaceans 84, 119

cucumbers 77

cumin seeds 56, 59

D

David, Elizabeth 180

deserts 164–168

dressings, salad 116–118

dried fruit 50

dried herbs 58

E

eggs 171

endive 78–79

entertaining 103–104

equipment 11

Eton mess 167

F

Fearnley-Whittingstall, Hugh 85

fennel 79, 109

fennel seeds 56, 59

fish 48–50, 79–84, 137–144

fish pie 144

fish stew 142–144

fish, tinned 49–50

flax seeds 56

fresh herbs 58

fridge 40–43

fried breakfast 169–170

fruit, tinned 50–51

fruit crumble 168

G

game, preparation 93–95

garlic 37–40

giblets 130

grains 46–47, 115

grapeseed oil 30

Gray, Rose 182

H

heat 97–99, 127

Henderson, Fergus 152

herbs, dried 58

herbs, fresh 58, 129

Himalayas 32

hollandaise sauce 161

I

ice cream 167

K

knickerbocker glory 167

knife sharpening 18–19

knives 16–19

knives, using 64–66

L

lamb 132
langoustines 122–123
larding 130–131
Lawson, Nigella 182
leaves, salad 68
Le Creuset 14, 15
leeks 71
lemons 34–36
lentils 46–47
linseeds 56
lobster 121

M

mackerel 141
Maldon, Essex 32
mangetout 72
marinades 88–89
marmalade 171–172
marrows 77
mayonnaise 161
meat, preparation 84–91,
   131–134
meat thermometer 24
molluscs 118–119
MSG 62
mushrooms 76–77
mussels 124

N

nigella seeds 56, 59

noodles 53–54
nuts 54–56, 115
nutmeg 59

O

octopus 141–142
offal 152–154
oil 28–31
oil, walnut 30, 117
olive oil 28, 29, 116
Oliver, Jamie 182, 183
Olney, Richard 182
onions 71
oysters 123–124

P

pans 12
pans, boiling 12–13
pasta 53–54, 149–151
pearl barley 52
peas 72
pepper 33–34
peppers 75
pestle and mortar 20–21
pie, fish 144
pine nuts 55
pistachios 55
polenta 52, 53
poppy seeds 56
pork 132
potatoes 70–71
pot roast 134–137
poultry, preparation 91–95

prawns 122–123
preserving 45
puddings 164–168
pumpkin 78
pumpkin seeds 56, 115
pulses 45–47, 115

Q
quinoa 52, 53

R
rapeseed oil 30
rice 52–53, 109, 144
rice pudding 166
risotto 144–146
roast dinners 125–134
roasting birds 128–131
roasting birds, larding 130–131
roasting birds, stuffing 130
roasting meat 131–134
Rogers, Ruth 182
root vegetables 69–70

S
salad 112–118
salad, Caesar 115
salad dressing 116–118
salad leaves 68, 114
salad, Spanish house 115
salad, Thai 115
salmon 82, 142
salsify 70
salt 31–33

sardines 141
sauces 159–162
sauce, béchamel 160
sauce, hollandaise 161
sauce, tomato 162
sauté pan 13–14
scallops 124–125
seafood, preparing 79–84,
    118–125
seasoning 56–60
sea salt 31
seeds 54–56, 115
Segnit, Niki 101
sesame oil 30, 115, 117, 118
sesame seeds 56, 118
shallots 71
shellfish 83–84, 118–125, 143
shopping 174–178
shrimp 122–123
Slater, Nigel 183–184
Smith, Delia 182
soup 104–111
soup, garnish 112
soy sauce 61–62
Spanish house salad 115
squashes 78, 109
squid 141
stews 134–137
stew, fish 142–144
stir-fries 155–156
stock 106–108
stuffing birds 130
summer pudding 166–167

sunflower oil 30
sunflower seeds 56, 115
sustainable fish 49, 79–80, 123, 125, 141, 142, 143, 148
swedes 70
sweets 164–168

T
Thai salad 115
tinned fish 49–50
tinned fruit 50–51
tinned vegetables 47
toast 146–149
tomatoes 73–74, 114
tomato sauce 162
tuna 49
turkey 128
turnips 70

V
vegetables 47–48, 156–159
vegetables, cooking 68–69
vegetables, preparing 66–69
vegetables, root 69–70
vegetables, tinned 47
vinegar 61, 117
vinegar, balsamic 61

W
walnut oil 30
walnuts 55, 115
wok 14, 155, 156
wooden spoons 22
writers, food 179–185